Search for Your Self

Search for Your Self

Pathways to Personal Growth

Dr. Patricia Sherwood

Floris Books

First published in 2010 by Floris Books

British Library CIP Data available
ISBN 978-086315-737-0
Printed in Great Britain
by Cromwell Press Group, Trowbridge

To the Sophia

Great wisdom mother within us,
May your light illumine our pathway to your
presence
Along the way.

That we be not deceived
By the delusions of power, greed and ignorance
Along the way.

May you awaken our insight and compassion to
discern that which truly heals us
Along the way.

All case studies in this book are composite profiles and do not refer to any single person living or dead. They are typical not individual experiences presenting in therapy.

Contents

Acknowledgments

To my students and graduates of Sophia College that they may continue to develop their insight and compassion in discerning healthy personal and spiritual growth

To my clients who have suffered upon the way in their quest for personal growth. May this book provide some signposts for guiding their journey.

To Martin who watered the seeds of my intention to write such a book.

And to all people everywhere who strive to create healthier ways of being in their lives. May their good intentions bear nourishing fruits along the way.

1. Personal growth: Which way?

As human beings
Our greatness lies not so much in being able to remake
the world
As in being able to remake ourselves.

— Gandhi

In 1970, at fifteen years of age, I remember walking into
the theosophical bookstore in Perth and asking for a book
about the purpose and meaning of my existence, and the way
to enlightenment. A bespectacled grey-haired lady who was
staffing the office at the time looked down at me and replied
stonily: 'If I had such a book, I would not be sitting behind
this desk today. I would be a very wealthy woman.' I learnt
quickly that volumes have been written on the subject from
both eastern and western viewpoints, and the challenge was
to discern which processes I would experience as promoting
my well-being and inner growth and clarifying what exactly
constitutes healthy personal growth

Today, the personal growth or self-help industry is one
of the fastest growing industries in the western world with
millions of books published and a multitude of bodily,
mental, emotional and spiritual processes being propounded
as the preferred way in magazines, businesses and festivals of
personal growth. In 2006, US$8.9 billion was the estimated
value of the industry in the United States alone. (www.

prosperyourmind.com). It is one of the fastest growing industries in the capitalist world and has vigorous proponents like Shirley McLean, Doreen Virtue, Anthony Roberts and vigorous opponents like Shermer who has named the movement SHAM (Self-help and Actualization Movement). He argues that there is no scientific evidence that any one option is better than another and that, in fact, none has been 'proven by science' (www.selfhelpwisdom.com). Salerno's invective is intense and he defines SHAM as:

> an enterprise wherein people holding the thinnest
> of credentials diagnose in basically normal people
> symptoms of inflated or invented maladies so that
> they may then implement remedies that have never
> been shown to work ... SHAM has filled the bank
> account of a slickly packaged breed of false prophets
> including but by no means limited to high profile
> authors, motivational speakers, self-styled group
> counsellors, life coaches and any number of wise men
> without portfolios who have promised to deliver some
> level of enhanced contentment. For a fat fee. (www.
> timesonline.co.uk. 6th January, 2008. Self-help Books?
> Don't bother. They won't help.)

He blames SHAM for the spate of divorces and for infecting everything from health care to education with false promises of helping people that result in doing little good. (Salerno, 2008). McIlwain (2006) reviews Salerno's book noting that few of his assertions are substantiated with any research evidence and that he fails to consider the very real needs of people that the personal growth industry may attempt to fulfil. He does not suggest other options that may meet the needs of people for more fulfilling lives, nor does he recognise that human growth is a continuous process, not something that is fixed.

Ardent proponents of personal growth programmes often promise outstanding benefits, including material wealth as espoused in books like Rhonda Byrne's The Secret (2006), interpersonal and romantic success, career and family benefits. The claims and counter claims, for and against personal growth processes, and the wide range of keenly marketed packages, challenges even the most discerning and insightful person. How does one define personal growth and how does one appraise the variety of options offered so as to eliminate those that are narcissistic, exploitative and useless, or a waste of time and money?

Eight of the major pathways to personal growth are explored throughout this book. These begin with processes focused more on the body, then primarily on the personal inner mental and emotional life, and finally on pathways that focus on the higher levels of consciousness and incorporate the transpersonal world, or connections beyond oneself. The pathways assessed and explored are:

1. Body as pathway;
2. Counselling as pathway;
3. Guru as pathway;
4. Psychics as pathway;
5. Guides as pathway;
6. Neo-shamanism as pathway;
7: Drugs as pathway;
8. Meditation as pathway.

The selection has been made on the basis of popular contemporary pathways found in the personal growth industry.

I do recognise that there are many traditional pathways to personal growth and/or spiritual awareness that include Vedic astrology, the Eneagram, Sufism, traditional religious practices and, although they are most worthy of review, they are not the focus of this book. Narcissism as roadblock on the pathway to personal growth is also explored because it is a critical feature in unhealthy psychological development in the personal growth movement today.

This book offers you clear criteria for assessing psychologically healthy personal growth. Clear outcomes and characteristics of healthy personal growth processes are established which derive from both psychological research on healthy personal growth and from a holistic model of human growth. This anthroposophically based holistic model of personal growth accounts for the material and non-material aspects of human experience, the mundane and extraordinary faculties of human beings, as well as their activities in both the secular and sacred worlds. This is essential if we are to appraise the diversity of contemporary pathways to personal growth in an embracing framework that can account for a human's personal-growth strivings, and aspirations to fulfil their highest potential.

Composite client case studies, drawn from holistic counselling practice are used to illustrate some of the potential pitfalls in each pathway. They provide examples of what can go wrong, not necessarily what will go wrong, because every pathway has its successes and in some pathways these far outnumber the failures. However, we learn most about the potential flaws in any field by examining what can go wrong. Then we begin to perceive clearly the boundaries of what is healthy in our pursuit of the search for ourself. Boundaries are found when we fall over the edge, not when we are happily settled in the centre. For that reason, I am focusing on case studies where personal-growth processes went wrong, rather than the multitude of successful case studies, so that we might cultivate wisdom to discern what are the features that promote healthy self-growth and what are the features that are unhealthily risky in the search for the self. In the words of Samuel Smiles (2008): 'We learn wisdom from failure much more than from success.' We often discover what we want by finding out what will not do. This book aims to define the boundaries of healthy personal growth and assists people make insightful decisions and critiques in choosing their personal-growth processes within a holistic framework, which embraces the fullness and diversity of human potential.

What is personal growth?

This is difficult to define but known in our experience as that feeling of body-soul-spirit vitality and well-being where we feel motivated to direct our lives so that we can manifest in the world the fullness of who we know we can be. We then feel deeply self-realized in our personal, social and vocational lives. Ryan and Frederick (1997:p.530) define this state as 'subjective vitality', which is the state of having positive growth-promoting energy available to control one's self and one's life direction. Such vitality is typical of a functioning person who experiences autonomy and the integration of their experience into a coherent self centre (Deci and Ryan, 1991). This is described by Rogers (1961) as the 'fully functioning person, and by Maslow (1968:p.173) as 'self-actualization'. Maslow characterizes self-actualizers as people who are centred on problems external to themselves, high on creativity, initiators of change, centres of meaning, open to experience, spontaneously expressive, capable of deeply loving relationships, accurate perceivers of reality, capable of great enjoyment, democratic, friendly, non-status oriented, have high levels of tolerance, compassion and philosophical humour with 'peak experiences' in which they experience self-transcendence. The outcome of this process towards self-actualization in any individual increases feelings of serenity, joy, confidence, zest for life, happiness, acceptance of others, confidence in one's abilities to handle stress and problems. (Maslow, 1959:p.127). Most importantly the self-actualizer's commitment to personal growth benefits others:

> The self-actualizer is not perfect but functions in growth-promoting ways in his/her world, so that there is a good correlation between subjective delight in the experience, impulse to the experience, or wish for it and basic need for the experience. Only such people uniformly yearn for what is good for them and for others and are able wholeheartedly to enjoy it and approve of it. (Maslow, 1959:p.129)

This profile describes well the outcomes of healthy personal growth, outcomes that are processes of realising ones' human growth potential. It is essentially about becoming who you uniquely are:

> A musician must make music, an artist must paint, a poet must write, if he is to be at peace with himself. What a man can be, he must be. This is the need one may call self-actualization ... It refers to man's desire for fulfilment, namely the tendency for him to become

actually in what he is potentially: to become everything that one is capable of becoming... (Maslow, cited by Leonhardt, 2008)

It is clear that personal growth is about increasing the quality of one's life as expressed by Abraham Lincoln: 'it's not the years in your life that count. It's the life in your years.'

In contrast, conflicts and demands on people that threaten their self-actualization and self direction, as well as loss of personal peace through fear, anxiety, panic, stress, anger, result in a person feeling a lack of effectiveness, lack of autonomy and a lack of relatedness. These diminish subjective vitality and well-being (Ryan, Deci and Gronick, 1995). Freud (1923) argued that the repression and unresolved conflict block the life drives of Eros. Despite different views and approaches to creating psychological well-being Jung (1960), Reich (1951), Perls (1973) Winnicott (1986), and Lowen (1968) all agree that the resolution of conflict, unauthenticity and self-fragmentation are essential for increased personal energy and vitality.

Another core element of personal growth is the need to initiate and carry on actions in our environment that result in the growth and flourishing of ourselves (White, 1960:100). A human being's primary psychological need is to be the origin of action in their world, and this basic need underlies intrinsic motivation and satisfaction in life (De Charms, 1968; Deci and Ryan, 1985). People experience high levels of positive subjective vitality when they experience themselves as the initiators, rather than the pawns of happenings in their lives.

Personal growth is about lessening the blocks and increasing the opportunities to take control of one's life destiny which increases one's personal vitality and well-being quite radically. This control begins by managing our reactions of fear and anger to events around us so that we are not buffeted by external events. Instead, we can maintain an integrated and empowered sense of self which creates a centre within us of peace and equanimity, regardless of external circumstances. Then from this position of an integrated and balanced self, we can effectively negotiate our way through environmental happenings and influence these by our thoughts, feelings and actions.

The central characteristics of healthy psychological growth and functioning have been summarized by Ryff and Singer (1998), who identify them as core dimensions of positive psychological functioning that promote holistic human flourishing. These are:

1. positive self-regard;

2. control and mastery over one's environment;

3. positive relations with others;

4. purpose in life;

5. autonomy;

6. positive experience: recovery and protective mechanisms.

These dimensions have been put into operation and measured by Ruff's psychological well-being scales and have formed the basis of several research studies to assess psychological well-being in people. One example is Lindfors (2002) survey testing positive health in a group of Swedish white-collar workers. Ryff and Singer (1998b) make the very important point that positive human health and well-being is focused on experiencing the above 'core life goods' that help keep people well. It is not about the pursuit of happiness, although happiness may be a byproduct of the 'core life goods'.

Characteristics of healthy personal growth

Based on the above psychological theories and research on healthy human growth that maximizes subjective vitality and well-being, I identify four core characteristics of any healthy personal growth process. These are:

1. Promotes the growth of the autonomous 'I'

When I am at the centre and have control and direction over the self-growth process and my self is strengthened by the process, then I can say that my 'I' is autonomous or self-governing. I am not subject to any process that I do not wish to be subject to and the process is explained adequately to me prior to me expressing an intention to undertake the process. This contrasts with unhealthy personal-growth processes where the client becomes more and more dependent on the facilitator and relies on them increasingly to direct life choices whether they are in relation to food, clothing, housing, relationships or work. This results in less and less self-autonomy and self-direction and more and more other direction and self-subjugation to somebody else's intentions. The overall consequence is to weaken the self or 'I' and reduce self-confidence, self-esteem and self- responsibility.

2. Emphasizes the client's capacity as initiator of processes

I can implement new ways of being and use new tools and techniques in my life to work with challenges. I am more able to make effective decisions free from pressure from others. My self-confidence is increasing in relation to personal growth, positive relationships with others, autonomy and purpose in life.

This contrasts personal-growth processes where the individuality of the client is overridden by decisions made by the facilitator, which reduces decision-making in the client's life. The client has less and less scope to act independently of the accepted reality propounded by the facilitator.

3. Provides processes so client can sustain improvements

Changes in the client's vitality and well-being can be maintained in the long-term and are not dependent on the facilitator in the long-term to initiate and maintain changes (autonomy, purpose in life, positive relationships with others). If the client becomes dependent on the facilitator to maintain and sustain positive changes it will involve long-term and regular expenditure of energy, time and money by the client to retain and maintain well-being. The length of the personal-growth process stretches from days and weeks to months and years without a corresponding increase in new techniques and tools being acquired by the client.

4. Monitors the client to ensure their 'I' can digest and integrate the experiences

Changes that arise in the personal growth processes occur at a pace that the client says: 'I can integrate these and I do not feel flooded or overwhelmed by what arises in my thoughts, feelings and actions. I have the tools to deal with what arises in relation to self-acceptance, autonomy, mastery of control over ones environment.'

By contrast, unhealthy personal growth triggers the client into emotional material or experiences that are not adequately processed or integrated into the client's experience. The client then feels that they lack tools or processes to deal with traumatic material and feelings that have been stimulated by the processes. If this occurs repeatedly, the client feels increasingly flooded and unable to function emotionally. In some rare cases, extensive flooding with traumatic material without the corresponding techniques to integrate it into experience will result in psychosis.

Summary of characteristics of Healthy Personal growth processes

1. Promotes the growth of autonomous 'I' or self.
2. Emphasizes the client's capacity as initiator of processes
3. Provides processes so client can sustain improvements
4. Monitors the client to ensure their 'I' can digest and integrate the experiences

Assess any proposed personal-growth process or package that you are considering undertaking in light of the above four characteristics and in terms of the following 4 outcomes if you want to increase your involvement in healthy personal growth, and minimize your involvement in psychologically unhealthy personal growth.

Outcomes of healthy personal growth

The four outcomes of healthy personal growth are:

1. I am more present to my daily life: body, mind and spirit. I live increasingly mindful of the present moment;
2. I am empowered to shape my destiny as I initiate and can direct my life experiences;
3. I am increasingly free from the reactions of fear,

anger, abandonment, emptiness and loss and instead
insight and compassion increasingly permeate my
being in the world;

4. I am more fully who I am — 'self-actualization' —
and am more capable of peak experiences of 'self-
transcendence' (connectedness).

Personal growth that has opposite characteristics and is
psychologically unhealthy is likely to be exploitative in one
or more ways: financially; emotionally; mentally; spiritually;
and socially. The four outcomes of unhealthy personal
growth are:

1. An increasing avoidance and disengagement
   from daily life routines and commitments, in the
   participants' intimate, social and work worlds. An
   increasing lack of awareness of day-to-day realities,
   and a desire to focus on other worldly ideas or the
   past, rather than the present moment. Living out
   of the past or living for the future but avoiding the
   present moment.

2. A weakening of the 'I' or self, by making it more
   and more dependent on the expert's knowledge or
   the expert's demands for allegiance to their way
   of being in the world that overrides the personal
   experience of the participant.

3. An enlarging of reactive states in the ongoing
   day-to-day life of the participant, which include
   one or more of the following: anger, rage, fear,
   abandonment, emptiness anxiety and panic. There
   is no decline in these reactive feelings nor an

increase in these reactive feelings over the length of the personal-growth process.

4. The diminishing of the unique individual's gifts and potential for some specified and restrictive formula of how one should be in the world, which is observable by a decline in the individual's ability to manifest the values of self-actualization, which include: joy, celebration, love, connectedness, creativity, truth, spontaneity, and the manifestation of one's unique gift in the world. Blocking the move to self-transcendence so the individual is not able to experience connections in ever-widening circles of relationships. Cutting off the access to the transpersonal dimensions of the human being that are characterized by compassionate relationships and connections to all beings.

Summary of the outcomes of healthy and unhealthy personal growth

Healthy personal Growth	Unhealthy personal growth
Fully present in the present moment	Focused on the past or the future
Empowered: initiates and makes own decisions	Disempowered: relies upon expert to make decisions for them
Enlarging states of equanimity and centredness	Enlarging reactive states of anger, fear, neediness, loss, emptiness, anxiety
Increased ability to manifest one's uniqueness	Conforming to other people's views of self
Increased connectedness and relationships in life	More isolated in relationships

A *holistic model for assessing healthy empowering personal growth*

This model sees a human being as comprised of body, soul and spirit and is the most appropriate model for assessing the range of personal-growth pathways because it provides a framework within which to understand and assess the range of personal-growth options. It also examines both processes grounded in the physical body and those located in human consciousness, as well as the relationship between material and spiritual experiences, between visible and invisible experiences in the personal growth field. Developed initially by Steiner in the 1920s, this is the foundation model of a human being used in anthroposophically based medical, nursing, counselling and education services. A directory of anthroposophical hospitals, clinics and services is contained in Evans and Rodger (1992) and Therkleston (2007). This model is represented diagrammatically opposite.

In this model, body, soul and spirit are the three main aspects of a human being, with body being the lowest vibration of the three. Body, soul and spirit themselves are each comprised of three sub-components.

The body

Body comprises physical body, etheric body and sentient body, the densest vibrational parts of a human being.

A holistic model of a human being and the thresholds of consciousness.
Source: Adapted from A Psychology of Body, Soul, Spirit Steiner (2000)

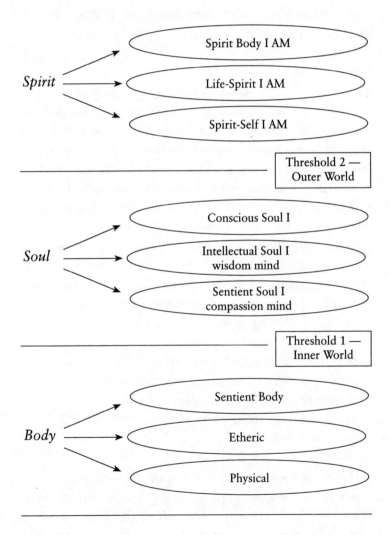

Physical body

The physical body is seen as the map of the mind and feeling states which are eventually lodged in the bodily cell memory as evidenced by the work of Pert (1997) and Borysenko (1994). This body is subject to the forces of gravity and is composed of elements of the mineral kingdom to which it will return upon death.

Etheric body

The etheric is a template of the physical body and directs the life processes of breathing, reproduction, metabolism, warmth, cell repair in the physical body (Steiner, 1997). Our physical body's vitality depends on this force. People vary in the strength of their etheric body, but it is strengthened by good eating, sleeping, rhythmical bodily patterns and contact with nature, particularly water sources, as it has a strong relation with the plant kingdom and the element of water (Therkleston, 2007:p.16). Physical, mental and emotional stresses drain it, as do lack of exercise, electro-magnetic radiation, irregular lifestyle patterns and contaminated and polluted air, water and food. Evans and Rodger (1992:p.33) describe the building up or anabolic nature of the etheric:

> [it is] the opposite to those [forces] of the physical
> world, where order degenerates into disorder.
> Wherever the etheric principle enters the physical
> world, it brings about order and from out of disorder
> and chaos.

Wherever there is fluid in the bodily system, there is the presence of the etheric force which interpenetrates every cell of the physical body. The etheric flow of energy is profoundly affected by our feelings and thoughts and acts as a mirror, reflecting them from the sentient body and sentient soul where they originate into the physical body. In eastern medicine it is the focus of medical practice such as homeopathy, acupuncture, acupressure, acutonics, johrei and reiki, because it is perceived that blocked energy in this field results in physical ill health and pain. It is particularly responsive to complementary therapies such as flower essences, aromatherapy and herbal medicine as it has an affinity with the plant kingdom. It is in essence the mainspring of our physical and emotional health and well-being.

Sentient body

This is the sensory survival instinctual body, akin to the animal body, where people are driven by their instinctual needs, their likes and dislikes, with no real awareness, insight or control over their behaviour. It is the body where the basic drives for food, water, shelter and sex emanate.

The soul

The human soul is akin to the notion of self in psychology but which Steiner (1991) terms the individuated 'I', which is the individual expression of creative consciousness or spirit. It is the unique experiences, talents and limitations of any human being. It is the place in which spirit interacts with the physical body through the senses. Contained within soul are all the sensory experiences of joy and trauma which are stored in the sentient soul. It also includes the higher order capacities of the human being, which include compassion and wisdom which can act together to transform traumatic and challenging experiences into the integrated or whole self. This is truly the arena for personal growth and all that occurs here is reflected downward into the body. This self or 'I' is like a bridge between the body and the spirit and comprises three dimensions.

Sentient soul

Sentient soul is the mediator with the sensory world of experience. It is the bridge into body and links into sentient body through the senses. It is the place where the impressions of the sentient body become incorporated into the permanent core of consciousness that is sentient soul. Together sentient body and sentient soul are labelled by Steiner as the 'astral'. It is the place where our day-to-day experiences of pleasure and pain are produced and stored. In Buddhism this is often termed the place of 'ordinary mind', to distinguish it from the place of 'insight' or higher mind states.

The astral has two parts: the sentient body and the sentient soul and it is between these two that the senses operate like hooks between the physical environment and the feeling dimensions of experience. It is sensory activity that provides the awareness connection through the senses, which links the soul with the physical body. Here, human experience based upon the senses is formed.

Many defence mechanisms emerge out of the struggle to survive and avoid pain on this astral level, as the experience is not always positive. Sentient soul is the place where all the imprints of our negative experiences — guilt, shame, trauma — are stored. As such it contains within it the trauma system of an individual's experiences if they have not been integrated through conscious awareness or insight. Sherwood (2004:20) terms these vibrational patterns 'imprints'. Many of our defence mechanisms merge out of our struggle to survive and avoid pain on this level. These mechanisms result in many aspects of experience being cut off, denied and suppressed. Buried experiences often run the life through the unconscious. This trauma system lacks integration with the self system or 'I', and consequently is responsible for most mental health problems (Steiner, 1999).

Sentient soul is the crucible in which, instead of allowing oneself to be driven by aversion and desire, sympathy and antipathy, one can work to cultivate compassion. When the duality between aversion and desire are transformed into compassion, when sympathy and antipathy are transformed into empathy, sentient soul is transformed into 'compassion mind'. The Dalai Lama is an exponent of this state of mind-soul which can only be achieved when one has freed self from reactions. As long as one experiences any anger, fear, resentment, irritation, annoyance, anxiety, agitation in one's mind, one has not yet fully transformed sentient soul into what is termed 'compassion mind' in Buddhism. This is the place of awakening; waking up to the mental prison of reactions which keeps one from true inner freedom.

This is the place in our day-to-day work in personal growth where we work to free ourselves from our aversion and our desires, to stop clinging to others to meet our needs, or blaming others for not meeting our needs. It is in this arena of the astrality that the keys to personal growth are embedded. Until we stop demanding that others satisfy our needs and reject those whom we dislike, our lives are driven by reactions to situations. We are not the driver of our own life in a proactive way that is so essential to personal growth, but rather are driving our lives reactively, always responding to the triggers around us and deeply dependent on the victim world-view that if only life was different, people were kinder and nicer we would be happy and free. We have given over ourselves to others to make us happy. We are bound to be disappointed, for this pathway does not lead to the fulfilled and flourishing self but rather a shrivelling, diminished flower of what our self potential might be. The first and biggest step to personal growth is to fully accept that we are responsible for our own mental and emotional states and that no one else can make us happy, angry, sad, disgruntled or agitated. This is the first step in the transformation of sentient soul to compassion soul/mind.

Intellectual soul

The second dimension of the soul is what is termed 'intellectual soul' by Steiner and is similar to the Buddhist notion of 'wisdom mind'. This is the seat of the thinking faculty. The intellectual soul permeates the sentient soul, and through thinking enables us to penetrate truths that go beyond our individual experience, everlasting truths that form wisdom and which Plato named as the 'ideal forms' or 'essences'. Reasoning is at the core of the wisdom which within intellectual soul transforms sensations of experience into knowing. If reasoning produces truth without any feeling or satisfaction for the soul, this leads to soul aridity, and the sterility that arises when intellectual soul is not warmed by feeling (Steiner, 1922:44). One of the most adverse consequences of this imbalance for personal growth will be detailed in Chapter 11 on narcissism as a pathway to personal growth.

Consciousness soul

Consciousness soul is the place in which we are freed from the activities of the sensory life so completely that we can see with clarity the essence of the 'I', the spirit (Steiner, 1997; 49). Through consciousness soul, we are united with spirit, the hidden element in everything manifest. In consciousness soul one realizes goodness, truth, justice, integrity, wholeness and the interconnectedness of all creation; the state which Thich Naht Hanh (1987) describes as the state of 'interbeing'. It is this realization within your individual life that provides the bridge to link the individual with the spirit, the place of interconnectedness and the realms of unity of consciousness which must be akin to Maslow's concept of the place of 'self transcendence'. Here the 'I', which in soul is the individuated manifestation of creative consciousness of spirit, bridges the spirit self, which is the place of the transpersonal creative consciousness or spirit, known in human religious traditions as the 'I AM'.

The Spirit

The highest layers of the 'I' manifest in the spiritual or realms of highest consciousness, form the 'I AM', and it is this transpersonal manifestation of creative consciousness which Steiner (1999) names 'spirit'. This is the eternal aspect of the human being as contrasted with the transitory temporal nature of the body. The spirit gives the soul its light, and the soul provides the space for things to be organized around the spirit and manifest in the physical world.

Spirit self

The spirit body provides a place for the 'I AM' to live and to perceive spiritual realities by means of intuitions. The elements of the outer spiritual world pulsate in it, and the spiritual world is communicated through 'spirit self' to consciousness soul as visions, inspirations and transcendent encounters. In 'spirit self' are the profound experiences where the boundaries of self dissolve and merge into patterns of infinite consciousness no longer enmeshed in the sensory attachments of the soul life. It is that which connects us to the transpersonal, essential to the experience of self-transcendence. This is akin to what Wilber (1975:p.107) describes as the doorway to the transpersonal where we discover all the universal 'higher order' values of love, beauty, goodness, justice, peace and compassion. Such an example is Frijof Capra's (1975) description of his vision of the dance of Shiva, when meditating on the beach one day. Everything including himself dissolved into particles of dancing energy; a grand interwoven symphony of consciousness and creative energy. The foundation for spirit self is the transformation of the soul life so that it is governed by wisdom and compassion. As such, at the point of spirit self, one may affirm that the Bodhisattva vows are becoming fully manifest as service governed by wisdom and compassion. Below is one example of these vows:

> All beings , I must set free
> The whole world of living beings I must rescue from
> the terrors of birth, of old age, of sickness of death
> and rebirth, of all kinds of moral offence, of all states
> of woe ... for with the help of the boat of the thought
> of all knowledge, I must rescue all these being ...
> (Skishasamkuccaya, verses 280f Vajradhavaja sutta.
> Conze et al, 1954:pp.131f)

Life spirit

This represents the high states where the creative life giving forces unconscious in the etheric body, become consciously engaged by the 'I' so that it participates in the creative realms of the 'I AM' (Steiner, 1997:p.54).

Spirit Body

Here, the 'I' or spirit has so infused and transformed the physical body it is indistinguishable from the spirit body. In the microcosm, this state has equivalents such as Atman in Hinduism, Buddha in Buddhism. Clinging to this individual microcosmic manifestation ignores the profound macrocosmic dimensions. Here, the individual manifestation of the spirit returns to the source of consciousness of the macrocosm, variously described in Hinduism as Brahma or the Paramatman, or in Buddhism as the state of Nirvana. Language struggles to capture this macrocosmic dimension:

> I will not call it coming and going, nor standing
> still, nor fading away nor beginning. It is without
> foundation, without continuation and without
> stopping. It is the end of suffering. (Tripitaka cited in
> Metz, 1982:p.234).

A human being is a profound meeting of body, soul and spirit: 'through the physical body, the soul is confined to physical existence; through the spirit body, it grows wings that give it mobility in the spiritual world' (Steiner, 1922:p.56). This leaves a human being designed and created as Alexander Pope in his famous Essay on Man captured so poetically: 'created half to fall and half to rise, the glory, jest and riddle of the world.' This is the great confounding dynamic underpinning the growth of a healthy integrated self.

The specific role of the 'I' in relation to body, soul and spirit

Steiner (1997) described the 'I' or insightful human consciousness which becomes the realized self, as the master of the etheric, astral and physical bodies and the seat of the self-aware human consciousness which has as its core defining feature, memory and insight. Within the 'I' are the archetypes of the human spirit, and the capacities to transmute painful experiences into growth and healing. It is the capacity of the human being to envision new realities out of reflection on past experiences, and to make choices so that instinctive behaviour and reactions, resulting from the astral body to increase pleasure and avoid pain, may be modified by higher motives such as compassion, empathy and justice (Evans & Rodger, 1992:p.49). It is the pace of insight. It brings the capacity to access resources of strength, courage, determination, love, joy and other qualities which Maslow (1973) named the 'B values or higher order values'. This 'I' is the individuated expression of spirit attempting to manifest in the human soul and body of a human being. It represents our greatest power and highest potential as a human being.

Psychological health and well-being depends on the capacity of the individual to insert their 'I' into their experiences and to integrate and process all experiences in a meaningful way so that no experience remains cut off, denied or repressed. (Sherwood, 2004:p.21). If this does not occur, then one's life remains driven by the astrality or the trauma system, rather than by skilful choices. The stronger the 'I', the greater the ability of a person to resolve emotional issues. The 'I' is strengthened by: practising focused mindfulness in daily activities; meditation practices that increase mindfulness and focus in daily life; developing clear intentions in one's life and following through on them; setting achievable goals and completing them; learning to identify emotional reactions based on fear, anger or loss and transforming them into equanimity. So one responds to the world increasingly from the position of insight and compassion rather than reaction.

Sherwood (2004) reiterates the important connection between the 'I' and the breath. Difficult experiences are imprinted vibrationally on the astrality which results in contraction of breath because it is painful to continue breathing into these places. This results in a removal of consciousness, or 'I', from the place of trauma which is repressed and hidden away from our consciousness by a defence mechanism. These are the parts of experience not embraced by the 'I' and which produce mental and physical disease and remain unintegrated in the trauma system or astrality. Abandoned by the 'I', these experiences often run the life in repetitive, depleting and unskilful ways driven by aversions and desires, flooding and repression, rather than by skilful choices and insight which generate energy.

Steiner describes the relationship between the physical, etheric and astral bodies and 'I', as dynamic, each interpenetrating the other:

The physical body would fall apart if the etheric body did not hold it together. The etheric body would sink into unconsciousness if the astral body did not illumine it. Likewise the astral body would repeatedly forget the past if the 'I' did not rescue this past and carry it over into the present. What death is to the physical body

and sleep to the ether body, forgetting is to the astral
body. We can also say that life belongs to the etheric
body, consciousness to the astral body and memory to
the 'I'. (1997:pp.39f)

Here, it is evident that the physical body requires the etheric,
the etheric the astral and the astral, the 'I', in this order.
The 'I' is the highest vibratory part of a human being so
that which occurs in the 'I' will eventually end up in the
physical body, given the basic principle that the higher
vibratory rate determines the lowest vibratory rate. What
emerges from our highest consciousness, intentions, will and
insight will ultimately run the show. Further details of the
interrelationship between these bodies are documented by
Steiner (1999) in Body, Soul and Spirit and Bott (1996) in
Spiritual Science and the Art of Healing.

Implications of this holistic model for personal growth

1. The autonomous 'I' is at the centre

The focus of healthy growth means that the autonomous
'I' of the individual is to be strengthened. In the degree
that the processes strengthens the individual's 'I', then in
that degree can the individual master the astral emotional
dynamics and transform them into skilful and productive
ways of being in the world. When the astral body is not
running out of control with aversions, desires, anger, fear
and loss then a healthy flow of breath can be maintained
which maximizes the etheric's capacity to maintain a
healthy physical body.

2. The 'I' consciously originates the change processes

It is essential that the personal growth processes originate in a very conscious intention of the 'I' to change in specific ways. Core to all successful personal growth is the conscious free-willed intention to change, to take responsibility for one's own mental state and to develop new and more functional ways of being in the world.

3. The 'I' is incarnated in the body to ensure that no other consciousness occupies the body

Personal growth processes must be tailored to increase the presence of the 'I' in the physical body, which can be monitored by the presence of the breath in every cell of the physical body down to the toes. The person becomes more present to day-to-day realities and the skills to manage them when insight increases. Processes that result in the 'I' becoming detached from the physical body and less present to the physical world are seen as excarnating and undesirable, as they leave the person vulnerable because when one's I is not in one's body; it is vacant for a new occupier or another form of consciousness such as disease, negative thought forms and in its extreme form, psychosis.

4. The 'I' is supported to access transpersonal resources

The 'I' at its highest level is a bridge to the transpersonal and can access resources from spiritual archetypes, the human world or the natural world and through processes of breathing, sensing, visualizing, sounding and gesturing can expand these resources to strengthen its capacity to deal with challenges and to transform traumas into strengths. Precise processes for achieving this are detailed in Sherwood (2007:pp.82–110).

5. The balance between anabolic and catabolic processes is monitored and maintained

It is essential in personal-growth processes to understand that emotional and mental trauma are catabolic processes that breakdown the life forces of the body to release mental and emotional energy. These astral, catabolic or breakdown processes of dealing with difficult emotional and challenging mental experiences are balanced by the etheric's anabolic or building-up capacities to maintain the vitality of the person. The level of the etheric vitality determines the person's energetic availability to work with the visible emotional/mental issues. When the etheric is depleted or run down, it will first need rebuilding through complementary health modalities prior to undertaking demanding astral work. Failure to do this can result in the collapse of the physical body through physical ill health, chronic fatigue illnesses and the like.

6. The astral experiences are only brought to the consciousness of the 'I' to the degree, and at the rate, that the person can digest and exit them on a daily basis

For balance in the whole organism, it is essential that emotional/mental traumatic material is processed as it is brought to consciousness to avoid experiences of flooding, which unnecessarily deplete the etheric and physical bodies and also lead the 'I' to leave the body through excarnation, and increase the person's vulnerability to emotional stress breakdown and physical health relapses.

7. There is integration between the personal growth experiences and the events and demands of daily life

It is essential in good quality personal growth to acquire tools and techniques that can be used for emotional first aid, to facilitate integration of what arises in personal growth with day-to-day events (Steiner, 1994:p.75) The client must be able to integrate personal growth into their daily lives if it is to be sustainable. Otherwise, the unintegrated material can cause flooding or the 'I' may withdraw from the body leaving the person ineffective in their daily world.

8. That a balance is maintained between thinking, feeling and willing (action in the physical world)

Here integration of a human being assumes that the person in healthy personal growth has the feeling life of the alive soul so that it warms and illumines the thinking processes with light, wisdom and a sense of interconnectedness to all life, and hence the thoughts are based on ethical foundations. The feeling life also infuses our actions in the world (willing) with compassion and awareness of the implications for other beings. We then become a human being with balance among our head, heart and body, the thinking, feeling and willing states of a healthy life. Smit (1989) documents a range of exercises designed to develop and balance thinking, feeling and willing.

Conclusion

This book offers you keys to unlock the complexities of the search for yourself; tools to navigate the pathways and criteria to assess different personal-growth options. Above all though, remember the test of any pathway to personal growth is the fruits it bears in your own experience and your own life. As the Buddha advised the Kalamas community:

Do not believe a thing because many people speak of it.
Do not believe on the faith of the sages of the past.
Do not believe what you yourself have imagined
Persuading yourself that a God inspires you
Believe nothing on the sole authority of your masters
and priests
After examination believe what you yourself have
tested and found to be skilful and conform your
conduct thereto.
(Snelling, 1992:3)

2. Quick fix or sustainable personal growth?

It is characteristic of wisdom not to do desperate things.
— Henry David Thoreau

Today it is all about speed, how quickly we can move, communicate, travel, eat and change as people and cultures. Daily we are pushed faster to keep up with a computerized, technological means of work and communication that works within seconds, and when we collapse we are offered immediate quick drug fixes for our tiredness, lethargy, grief and loss, depression and other mental and bodily malaise. The prescriptive drug industry is booming, In 2002, the Fortune 500's ten drug companies had combined profits of US$ 35.9 billion, surpassing the total profits of the remaining 490 firms (Goldstein, 2004). Economically, quick growth at any cost to the environment is the dominant policy, so we can now have the material things that we want endlessly. Most of us travel through life in the fast lane, until physically or emotionally we breakdown, burn out or manifest chronic fatigue. And then there is the crisis of being overtaken in the competition for more, more, more. It is not surprising that we develop a psychological ethos where we are attracted by 'quick-fix' personal growth. It covers a vast range of diversified products, processes, seminars and books within the personal-growth field that promise major transformations with minimal personal investment, often in as little as one encounter. Why engage with the self or 'I' in in-depth psychological growth processes to create and sustain a healthy life change when a drug or a quick one-off intervention can eliminate the problem? Or so the marketers tell us. The lure of speed in personal growth is great. It is compatible with the fast-paced economic and social systems in which we live our daily lives.

Going slower, taking more time to heal, to grow and recover is not readily compatible with the multitudes of demands on our life. Yet we need to be aware that the healthy rhythm in our human body, is the rhythm established by regular full breathing and is reflected in the etheric body. Speed overrides this rhythm and creates stress in the etheric. When the etheric is weak and depleted, then serious emotional trauma vibrates directly from the astral layers into the physical body, manifesting in a range of mental and physical health problems. Usually our major health collapses are when we are both physically and emotionally stressed and depleted. In fact, it is when the astral, catabolic or break-down processes exceed the capacities of the etheric or anabolic building-up processes that we become really exhausted. We are literally in energetic debt and become ill (Sherwood, 2007). Too much mental work or too much emotional work arising from ill-considered speeded-up personal-growth processes can also trigger this imbalance.

The promised benefits of quick-fix personal growth options

Quick-fix packages for personal growth range from high-tech material interventions to the most abstract energetic interventions and usually promise instant relief from, or solutions for, pressing physical, mental, emotional or psychological problems without us having to engage our will or 'I' in a substantial way. On the surface it saves time, and in western society we are individually and socially short of time for relationships with self and our families, even though family has been rated as the most important quality affecting our happiness (Layard, 2005:p.63). Often the quick-fix pathway to personal growth appears as a relatively cheap option because one is only going to need one or two visits for the problem to be solved. It feels like a relatively painless approach. One is not required to dig deeply into the imprints in one's soul (astrality) which is the root of the presenting problem, nor work to heal these patterns. Instead there is an attraction in being able to ignore them, keep them locked away and repressed and still solve the problem, albeit quickly. It is a sort of emotional bypass where we passively acquiesce in the process of superficial personal growth, but it is built upon shaky foundations of our unintegrated and often repressed personal traumas. So why does the quick-fix option so often disappoint many people and not regularly deliver the results they expect, particularly in the medium and long-term?

The hidden costs of the quick fix:

Unsustainability

The 'quick-fix' personal-growth packages target the market of busy people who are unlikely to have the time to examine deeply the integrity of the packages offered or to research the possible outcomes, or who simply want another perspective on a difficult problem that promises to be economical and on time, not realising that it has neither long-term sustainability, nor does it strengthen their self-growth. It is part of the western syndrome of 'getting fixed up' by external forces when something goes wrong rather than actively engaging one's insight in diagnosis and interventions to recover one's self. Essentially, it is letting someone else drive the vehicle of your life rather than you driving it and improving your driving skills with assistance and information from informed and experienced others. You are a passenger in your vehicle of life rather than the driver, and it supports the dependent, disempowered role in your life if it is used often as your preferred pathway to personal growth. Sustainability refers to whether the changed behaviour lasts in the short-term (days and weeks), the medium-term (months) or the long-term (years). This is the litmus test of quick-fix personal-growth programmes and while people may report short-term changes, are these sustained in the medium or long-term? Unless the 'I' or place of insight is actively engaged it is unlikely that the change will be sustained in either the medium or the long-term.

It is important to understand that even when we effect changes in our astral or soul experiences, such changes do not easily become part of our character or temperament unless these are integrated into the etheric body. This is the body of rhythm where habits, good and bad, echo in rhythms and underpin the physical and astral bodies. Steiner insightfully expounds this integrated process of change:

> It is not possible to draw a fixed boundary between the changes that take place s a result of the activity of the I in the astral body and those that take place in the etheric body, since they blend into each other. If something we learn enhances our faculty of judgment, a change has taken place in the astral body, but if this judgement changes our state of mind so that we become accustomed to feeling differently about a subject after having learned about it, then a change has taken place in the ether(ic) body. Everything we take possession of in such a way that we can recall it again and again is based on a change in the etheric body. Anything that gradually becomes an entrenched part of the wealth of our memory rests on the fact that the work performed on the astral body has been transferred to the etheric body. (Steiner, 1997:pp.52f)

The transfer from the astral to the etheric body to create sustainable change cannot be done in the short-term, quick-fix model. It takes time to consolidate the change in the etheric and this is achieved through repetition on a daily, weekly and monthly basis, through artistic activities that bring the new energy into the etheric, and through daily noble religious practices such as meditation, chanting, praying and uplifting rituals.

Finally, many personal-growth courses attempting dramatic personal changes in short periods of time have trainers who use psychological processes without adequate in-depth training and little awareness as to the possible consequences of the interventions. In particular, Samways (1994:p.41) mentions the misuse of hypnotherapy and associated techniques by practitioners with inadequate training or qualifications, and without indicating to participants exactly what they are doing.

Another example is meditation machines. Short-cut technological machines to speed up the natural processes of acquiring the experiences of meditation have some problems. For example, the PDT Inner Brain Quest claims to provide short cuts to relaxation, creativity and high mental performance. It aims to stimulate the higher mind states saving the client hours of meditation practice or body-based counselling to restore the natural heart-lung rhythms, undertaken effortlessly in a short space of time. This machine aims to manipulate the subject's brain-wave state through the application of sound and light patterns. The subject wears headphones and dark glasses connected electronically to a machine which generates white noise and audio tones together with light flashes inside the spectacles. After 15–45 minutes it is hoped that the brain will be reprogrammed into a state synchronicity which maximizes its capacity to accept new information and experience deep relationships (Fox, 1990). On completion of a one-hour session, one should leave feeling relaxed and more creative in one's ideas. This machine certainly has benefits which some people experience in their bodies and minds. However, it has significant limits if we critique it in light of the characteristics of psychologically healthy personal growth and compare it to client-directed meditation practices.

In the case of the Inner Brain Quest machine, for example, the technology acts temporarily as a substitute for the integrated self or 'I' and one does not build up the internal muscles within one's own mind, which become dependent on a machine to induce the state of relaxation. This limits the transferability of the benefits to different situations and may restrict one to being relaxed only when one has access to a machine. Also because a machine is an artifice, not identical to the natural flows of the etheric, in some people it may result in unpredictable physical side effects and is likely to aggravate anyone prone to epilepsy or who is light-sensitive. While promoters of this product may state that it should not be used by people under the influence of drugs or alcohol, or with diagnosed epilepsy, seizures, heart conditions, or a psychiatric illness, this does not address the very real problems of people who have not been diagnosed but are suffering from any of the above (Fox, 1990). Once triggered into a negative episode, it is difficult to exit, as the 'I' or integrated self is not the locus of control which has been abandoned in favour of the quick-fix technology. While this triggering may occur in only a small percentage of cases, if you are the person adversely affected then, experientially, for you and your life, there is no comfort in knowing you are part of 2% of the population adversely affected. In addition, in the case of the Inner Brain Quest machine, repetitive usage seems to be required and some people even invest substantial amounts of money in buying their own personal machine to keep them calm. The quick fix offer can turn into a long-term investment in a machine and one must ask: How does the person maintain these mind states when they cannot access their machine? Here the sustainability of the experience of change in mental processes is not high. The body does not lie, nor does the breath so this is one way of monitoring the effectiveness of such a quick fix package upon your bodily organism. Also one must ask what are the unanticipated side effects of such an invasive process on the brain energy patterns. Some people cannot digest rapid light stimulation and may become disoriented or confused, fell weak and shaken. How do you check if you are one of these people and what back-up is there for clients who experience the sounds and lights adversely? In the case of the Inner brain quest machine, for example the technology temporarily acts as a substitute for the integrated self and one does not build up the internal muscles within one's own mind but becomes dependent on a machine to induce the state of relaxation. This limits the transferability of the benefits to different situations.

The holistic model of body, soul and spirit from a lifespan developmental perspective

Personal growth opportunities are also circumscribed by age, particularly because maturity has a great deal to do with ability to initiate and direct personal change. This nine-fold model (see diagram on p. 52) assumes that there is an incarnation process whereby the individual spirit or consciousness entering into manifestation in the physical body takes 21–28 years to incarnate and to be fully present as a mature human being. Lievegoed (1997) in Phases of Childhood details this developmental model. The first 7 years are devoted to the growth of the physical body, the second 7 years to the etheric, 14–21 years is devoted to the incarnation of the astral with the emergence of full adult sexuality; and 21–28 to the full incarnation of the 'I', or the individual unique manifestation of consciousness or spirit in the world. The period of 21–42 years is devoted to the full manifestation of soul in the world, while the period of 42–63 years is the period for the manifestation of a person's mature spirit in their life and the world. Because the spirit demands the fullest potential of a person, after 42 years one cannot engage healthily in occupations or relationships that are not fully meaningful and authentic for the self. One cannot live for tomorrow, one must live to manifest fully today. This adult developmental model, underpinned by the ninefold model is elucidated by Lievegoed in Phases (1996).

The psycho spiritual push for personal growth accelerates after 28 years and is strongest in the post 42-year period. As Jung (1960) noted there is more psycho-spiritual energy available for the cultivation of wisdom as people age especially after a person has completed the developmental tasks of bearing, raising and maintaining a family. People have the potential to mature psychologically with age and generally report higher levels of well-being than younger people. (Sheldon & Kasser, 2001). Jung (1960) also noted that from mid-life onwards there is greater psychological capacity to own who one is, to develop who one is as a person, and to address one's shadow or unknown qualities as well as one's known qualities. This contrasts with earlier ages where it was easier to project our un-met needs and un-owned parts of ourselves onto other people, particularly intimate partners. This is very unskilful and results in harsh judgements of self and others which are not conducive to positive subjective vitality and well-being. With aging comes the psycho-spiritual energy to invest in personal growth and to integrate all parts of self so one may be more fully present in one's life and vocation. From forty-two years onwards, personal growth is a must if one is to experience a high quality of life, personal vitality and well-being. The question becomes not 'should one undertake personal growth', but rather 'what type of personal growth will maximize my well-being and vitality in my intimate, social and vocational life?'

What hinders personal growth across the lifespan?

The core block to personal growth occurs during the incarnating phase as the unique individual 'I' comes down through spirit into soul and enters through the senses in the astral to link with the sensory world (the interface between body and soul). Here, it experiences traumatic, threatening, cooling or brutally invasive forces directed towards it or others that cannot be digested by the immature 'I' of the infant or child. To survive, the child places defence mechanisms around the experiences in sentient soul which repress, sublimate, and deny the experience. The 'I' consciousness together with the breath withdraws from those places, and they form contractions in the astral body, places where the experience ceases to be consciously known. These contractions act as blocks to the realization of one's full potential in adult life.

Over and under-incarnated responses

Overly incarnated

Some individuals chose to avoid living in the sentient soul by becoming overly incarnated and living their lives out of the body alone which includes the physical, etheric and sentient or instinct body. Such individuals are said to be over-incarnated and are usually preoccupied with material experience and are prone in their excesses to greed, cruelty, misuse of sexuality and misuse of material power. They have difficulty accessing their feelings, lack empathy and are blocked against accessing the qualities of the higher soul and spirit including imagination, intuition, and inspiration as well as being cut off from the experience of intimacy and interconnectedness. Often they are lonely exiles from their hearts and intimacy which they compensate for with money, sex or excessive materialistic experiences. They avoid going to their feelings located in sentient soul at any cost and their defence mechanisms are usually strong.

Under-incarnated or excoriated

In contrast, other children who experience emotional trauma in the sentient soul as they incarnate withdraw and locate themselves above sentient soul, often in intellectual soul. This survival mechanism of avoiding pain in the sentient soul leads to under-incarnation whereby the person is prone to excesses of the imagination, thinking and dreaming. These people are often overly empathetic, have poor boundaries and difficulty being grounded in the material world and in manifesting their vocation in the world. Their personal growth is stunted by their severance from the body and their exile in intellectual soul. Often these types of people talk excessively about feelings without allowing themselves feelings, or they are unable to keep other people's feelings out of their personal space.

Whether over- or under-incarnated, aspects of experience are consigned to the unconscious in sentient soul, forgotten and they block personal growth despite the best intentions of some people for personal change. These repressed experiences cannot be accessed easily by the individual by talking or thinking about them. Rather bodily processes must be used to bring the memories from the body cells and astrality to consciousness. Often people sense something is blocking their efforts and then, without adequate tools to access these astral imprints with their own 'I', they become vulnerable to, and dependent on, psychics, guides, mediums, shamans and gurus to uncover the hidden information. Literally, they hire outsiders to read the book of their own soul experience and are vulnerable to the integrity, accuracy and agenda of the outsider. The process may be quick, but it can be very costly for the overall personal well-being of the person seeking personal growth. When access to astrality is not directed by one's own 'I', what arises is likely to create problems in terms of digestibility and sustainability, as well as expose the person's soul history to a motley collection of soul doctors, many without credentials or with questionable ethics.

The personal growth thresholds

As can be identified in the above diagram of the holistic human being, there are two thresholds; one between body and soul, and one between soul and spirit. These thresholds represent the need for major inner strength and inner psycho-spiritual skills to digest what can arise when crossing them. Steiner argues that a process exists to support individuals traversing these thresholds. He identifies the lesser guardian (threshold 1) and great guardian (threshold 2) as the metaphoric assistants that do not permit an individual to traverse these places unless they are adequately prepared and skilled to deal with what arises on the other side of the respective threshold. They govern the appropriate time to traverse these thresholds when the individual self can healthily digest and integrate

the experience that arises from crossing the threshold
(Steiner, 1994:pp.184–87). These guardians are the bearers
of our highest self-wisdom.

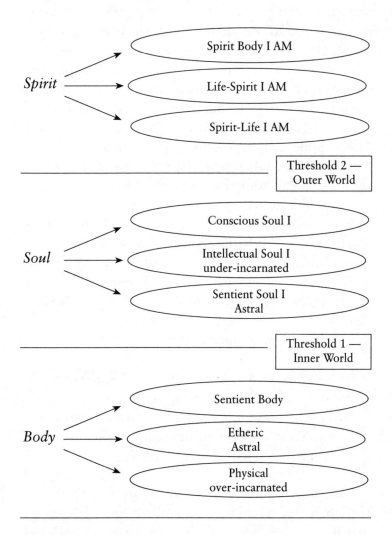

Threshold 1: Awakening to self: Uncovering, transforming and integrating ones experiences

This is the threshold of stepping into sentient soul, to become familiar with all of your experiences, however traumatic, whether as perpetrator or victim, saint or sinner, prostitute or virgin, angel or devil. Across this threshold one meets one's own shadow from all previous cellular memories, past lives or aspects of one unconscious, however one chooses to name it and process it. Here is revealed the black, white, grey and coloured qualities of ourself in all its moments of glory, misery, triumph, defeat, pride and humiliation. Guilt and shame can be pervasive feelings having crossed this threshold without adequate preparation to re-experience these parts of our shadows. It is essential we cross the threshold with a mastery of the processes of self-forgiveness. Channellers, psychics, mediums and gurus may penetrate another person's threshold one and reveal information to the individual prematurely, which can create serious psychological disturbances for the unprepared individual. Steiner cautions us to listen to the voice of the guardian of this threshold who commands us:

> Do not cross my threshold until you fully understand
> that you yourself have to illuminate the darkness
> before you Do not take a single step forward until you
> are absolutely sure that you have enough fuel in your
> own lamp ... (Steiner, 1990:p.193)

The individual must be fully resourced with positive archetypes that one can access for courage, power, and strength whether drawn from the cannon of goddesses, gods, great religious traditions or indigenous or ancient traditions of meaning. It is in crossing this first threshold with adequate preparation that we integrate our own shadows into ourselves, and for the first time begin to embrace and integrate the whole self, which creates the foundation for compassion in the world and the fulfilment of our highest vocational destiny.

Lievegoed (1985:p.94) terms this 'the guardian of the lesser threshold'. He proposes that this guardian representing the 'sum total of our negative past' was protected from our consciousness until the later part of the twentieth century. With the thinning of this threshold in recent decades, people are increasingly half conscious of the material that was previously so effectively cut off from their consciousness. Such half consciousness, he suggests, is behind the feelings of depression, fear, repulsion, shame and disgust. This lesser guardian he describes as bearing the countenance of all our accumulated thoughts, feelings, desires, actions and deeds.

Threshold 2: Awakening to inter-being and the Bodhisattva vows

At this threshold between soul and spirit, we are freed from the bondage of the sensory world (Steiner, 1997:pp.202–205). Our thinking, feeling and willing, are no longer attached to aversions and desires, and are freed to be mobilized by the 'I' for the great well-being and benefit of all beings. As we cross this threshold we manifest our Bodhisattva vows: 'As long as space remains; As long as sentient beings remain, until then, may I too remain, and dispel the miseries of the world.'

This is the ultimate destination of personal growth and is dangerous unless profound inner work has been effected by the 'I' through the soul life of the sensory world. Too many people have gone there in a hurry only to find madness, dissociation and psychosis. Also, if the person is not adequately prepared with skills and knowledge about this threshold, the feelings of bliss, release from day-to-day cares, a sense of liberation from bodily constraints, and at times ecstatic feelings can lead to a range of addictions in an attempt to repeat crossings of this threshold purely for personal indulgence (Lievegoed, 1985:p.143). The end of the addictive journey is not only the loss of bliss and ecstasy but the breakdown of the physical and etheric bodies, sometimes to the point of death. At other times, 'bad trips' fail to send one across the second threshold of excarnation. Without a driver or 'I' presence, the beings encountered in this realm, while always powerful, may not be beautiful. Terrifying forms and beings give people 'bad addictive trips'.

The key to sanity and skilfulness in the crossing of the second threshold is to remain devoted to the Bodhisattva path which is the commitment to manifest one's gifts, insights and abilities derived from one's inner work in the sensory world, for the benefit of all beings while still remaining in the sensory world. It is only the altruistic gesture of the Bodhisattva that ensures that one remains safe in the crossing of this threshold. Santideva describes the altruism of the Boddhisattva:

> May I become medicine for the sick and their
> physician, their support until health comes again;
> May I become an unfailing store for the wretched and
> be first to supply them with the manifold things of
> their need.
> My own self and my pleasure, all my righteousness,
> past, present and future, I sacrifice without regards,
> in order to achieve the welfare of all beings (cited in
> Hewage, 1997:p.18)

Without selfless devotion to the service of others, one risks the temptations on the Mount, where power and glory are offered for self-aggrandizement. This is a detour to narcissism, one of the great dead-end pathways to personal growth in the twenty-first century.

Across this threshold is the supersensible world of the pure forms of light, sound, movement and colour that overwhelm those who have not had adequate preparation in the soul life in the sensory world. It is across this threshold that drugs, trances, shamanic rituals may take us, but these personal-growth pathways are fraught with danger if our 'I' has not adequately been prepared through the mature growth of its thinking, feeling and willing life in the sensory world, and its devoted service along the pathway of the Boddhisattva. Across this threshold is the world of form merging into formlessness, where all mingles in a vast space of consciousness and where the boundaries to which we cling to define ourselves dissolve into a pervasive oneness. In the words of the great Buddhist Prajna Paramita chant, also known as the Perfection of Wisdom

> ... Form does not differ from the void. And the Void does not differ from form. Form is void and void is form. The same is true for feelings, perceptions, volitions and consciousness ... (Lok To, 1995)

The different pathways to personal growth will also be assessed in light of the sustainable skills they offer to navigate one or both of the thresholds of personal growth as elucidated above.

Below is a case study of a quick-fix option where the client consulted an energy guide who claimed to be able to see into the client's interior life. The client was vulnerable in exposing herself to someone else's perception and penetration of threshold one of the client's life. It is an excellent illustration of the lack of sustainability potentially inherent along the quick-fix route. Quick knowledge may weaken rather than strengthen the person, particularly if their 'I' is not engaged in the process of uncovering the knowledge beyond the first threshold of incarnation.

Case study

The primary case study drawn from therapy for the 'quick fix' scenario is a forty-three-year-old woman, Mary, who is reflecting on a career change. She is uncertain whether to leave her long-term professional career in the university sector and move into a private consulting business with her partner and is tired of the indecision. Mary is highly intelligent, deeply appreciative of the arts, cultured and sophisticated. She has no mental health history and until recently, despite her slender build had been very robust, working twenty-hour days for the past twenty years with only three days sick leave during that period of time. She is a very competent woman with a successful career, confident in her abilities and happy mother to three children aged two, five and eight, and a partner whom she helps in his business when her working day finishes. However, in recent times she has noticed that her vast reservoir of energy seems to be draining away and she often feels tired and wakes up exhausted. She has been pushing herself to work by sheer willpower and this has increased her reflections about changing her employment and reshaping her lifestyle. After speaking to several of her friends about her career dilemma, they recommended an energy-based intuitive guide with whom two of them have had positive sessions in reviewing their life directions and making quick decisions.

Mary attended a one-hour session with the intuitive healer to obtain a quick clean resolution to her career choice. At the beginning of the session, Mary clearly stated that she wished to gain more insight on her career-move dilemma. This wish was ignored by the intuitive practitioner who proceeded to inform Mary that she had cancer and unless immediate action was taken to relinquish all her work commitments she would probably die within three months. In addition, she told Mary that the property she owned would be sold within the year and her relationship with her current partner would break up within the next few months, and that Mary could expect a period of chaos in her life. She then concluded the session and left Mary in a state of shock. Mary then went to her car to drive the sixty kilometres to her next appointment. On the way she was stopped by two police for speeding. When they asked Mary did she know how fast she was going, she replied 'no' and when they asked her did she know where she was, Mary could not identify the road or location in which she was driving. The police become concerned about her lack of presence and asked her what was wrong. She broke down crying saying that she had just been told that she had cancer and she did not want to die as she had three small children to care for. One of the police then drove her to her next appointment and ordered her to visit a medical doctor the next day and fax him a signed copy from the doctor saying that he had examined her for cancer, otherwise she would be given a speeding ticket.

The next day Mary dutifully arrived at the doctor's surgery in tears, and told him the prognosis from the intuitive healer's session. The doctor had a range of tests undertaken and within a week cleared her of cancer but instead diagnosed chronic fatigue and burnout. Mary was given leave from work for one month that extended eventually to three months as she worked with her chronic fatigue so she could re-enter the workplace. However, she also undertook six sessions of somatically-based counselling to deal with her fear, shock and grief that had arisen as a consequence of her visit to the intuitive healer.

This case will now be reviewed in light of the outcomes of healthy personal growth to highlight some of the problems of the one-off 'quick-fix' session, in which someone else crosses the first threshold of the client's interior life and makes predictions with levels of inaccuracy.

Summary of the outcomes of healthy and unhealthy personal growth

1. I am more present in my daily life
Mary was so shocked from the sudden very bad news about her health, which as it turned out was inaccurate, that she was relatively dissociated for a week after the energy intuitive session, until she received news that she did not have cancer. It is true that she was not well and the session confronted her with that fact, but shocking news given in one session, no matter the accuracy of it or not, usually leads to dissociation for most clients who have no support to digest and integrate the shocking news into their experience.

2. I am empowered to shape my destiny
The client's wish or original intention to discuss her career options was completely ignored. Instead, she was given a great deal of information about other aspects of her life

that she had not requested and the information proved to be incorrect and unnecessarily distressing. Mary felt her life and destiny had suddenly become out of her control and she found this very disempowering. The client was given no support to access resources that might give her strength to deal with the life-threatening predictions of the energy intuitive. This left her alone in her distress.

3. I am increasingly free from reactions

The energy intuitive's dire predictions about several aspects of Mary's life triggered in her intense feelings of fear, abandonment and loss, rather than increase her ability to function with centredness and calmness in her life. Mary's levels of reactions and emotional flooding increased rather than declined after the session with the intuitive healer. The amount of astral material presented to the client about her life, her health, her personal relationship and her property was all based around losses and, even if it had been accurate, it was too much for the client to assimilate and integrate into the functioning self in one hour.

4. I am more fully who I am: 'self-actualization' and 'self-transcendence'

Mary did not feel she gained any insights that helped her become her self more fully. On the contrary, her confidence and self-esteem were shaken by the abundance of negative comments and the absence of positive comments or encouragement about her abilities As a result, Mary's social relationships diminished as she retreated into herself to recover from her shock. To understand why the energy intuitive failed to support the client achieve any of the outcomes of healthy personal growth, we need to place it in context of the holistic model of personal growth.

The holistic model of personal growth for body, soul and spirit: The consequences

This quick fix provides attractive packages with promises of rapid change for little investment in time. However, the human spirit or highest consciousness, the 'I', must be engaged for the change processes to be sustainable in the long-term. The self needs time to develop insight and, through conscious awareness, to integrate new patterns of thinking, feeling and acting. Quick-fix packages do not often actively engage the 'I' in transforming and releasing the difficult energetic patterns which remain hidden from the conscious mind and still operate through the bodily cell memory. Jung (1960) accurately indicates, that that which remains repressed in the unconscious, will eventually drive our lives. It will be responsible for many of our shadow behaviours and repetitive personally destructive behaviours, particularly self-sabotage, self-righteousness and self-condemnation. Quick-fix approaches too often treat the human being like a machine to be readjusted or repaired with a new part, whereas a human being's life and experience is like an intricately woven tapestry full of many different colours and hues, knitted together by enmeshed patterns of experience. One cannot pull a thread without the whole tapestry of one's life being altered. Personal growth has a broad vision that sees the whole tapestry, not just the single thread of the presenting issue. When the whole picture is seen, the 'I' is engaged to integrate the change and this takes time and repetition so that the change becomes a new habit.

When we are in overdrive, beating the clock, our breathing is shallow and we know we are not living the quality and fullness of life of which we are capable. We see only a thread in the tapestry and fail to notice we are an intricate interwoven tapestry with many interconnections, all parts influencing the whole. We make more errors and life has less satisfaction and our needs become unending. Thinking dominates feelings, our natural bodily breathing rhythm, and in overdrive we clutch at the quick-fix solutions, without appraising them adequately to separate out the wheat from the chaff. We need to need to slow down and review the implications for the whole tapestry of pulling one thread. If we are to undertake personal growth skilfully and sustainably we need to remember Thich Naht Hanh's caution that: 'There is not much time, therefore we must go slowly.'

3. Body as pathway

The body isn't simply there to carry the head
—Candice Pert

At last, western culture has discovered the body as a
pathway to personal growth and the body is core to a
burgeoning number of contemporary personal-growth
processes such as New Linguistic Programming (NLP),
rebirthing, holiotropic breathwork, somatic therapies,
thought-field therapies, emotional freedom therapy,
kinesiology, core energetics, neuro-emotional technique,
theta healing, network chiropractic and shiatsu. However,
the body-mind connection is not new and Reich (1973), a
contemporary of Freud, wrote prolifically on the subject
seeing blocked emotional/psychic energy as reflected in
contracted muscular energy in the body. He developed a
number of character structures based on body gesture which
he could use to predict particular emotional states and
experiences (Eiden, 2002:pp.28–35). Lowen (1990:p.35)
used breathing and body exercises to release a range of
emotional experiences, and Pierrakos (1990) founded core
energetics which also included the etheric or subtle body,
and the 'I', which he named the spiritual body so that it
embraced the whole human being. He incorporated the use
of chakras into his model of personal growth. Pierrakos's
model of core energetics is very holistic.

All emotional/ mental 'astral' experiences have energetic resonances in the cellular structures of the body. Pert describes this insight developed from her ground-breaking work in the 1980s in locating the opiate receptors on cell walls:

> The molecules of our emotions share intimate
> connections with and are indeed inseparable from our
> physiology. It is the emotions that link mind and body
> ... the molecules of emotion run every system in our
> body ... (Pert, 1987:p.18)

Walter Russell elaborated upon this concept showing how physical health is so dependent on the nature of our thinking:

> ... a single thought can change the polarity of our
> entire body toward either life or death — and can
> likewise change its entire chemistry toward increasing
> alkalinity or acidity to strengthen it or weaken it — or
> can change the shape of every corpuscle of matter in
> the entire body in the direction of either growth or
> decay ... (Staunton, 2002: p.147)

Vick, cited in Staunton, is an active proponent of noting the impact of our thoughts on our lives. He proposes that the mindfulness practice of being focused on the present moment through monitoring ones breathing is a primary method for bridging into the traumatic material stored in the body and releasing and transforming it. Totton, (2003:pp.88-116) identifies twenty-five different approaches that have been developed to deal with the somatic relationship between body and mind which he broadly categorizes in terms of three models including the adjustment (Bio-energetics), trauma (rebirthing), and process (Gestalt) models.

In terms of meeting quality standards, there are now many somatically based professional associations in counselling, psychotherapy and complementary health that set training standards for many different modalities. When assessing quality, it is important to ask whether the practitioner training is accredited 'in-house', that is by the provider only, or whether it is accredited by a national professional body. While national accreditation does not always eliminate all the incompetent or unethical practitioners, it does minimize them and ensures that you have a professional body to refer to, should any grievances arise. In-house accreditation is less likely to identify incompetent and unethical practitioners.

The promised benefits

Body as pathway promises a holistic pathway to personal growth that embraces the whole of the person (Totton, 2003:p.62) It can work quickly and efficiently with what is really going on because the cellular memory of the body will release it to the conscious mind through a range of techniques One is not simply relying on words and memory in the conscious mind so that progress can be quick because information is gleaned from bodily gesture, tone and the client's energy levels. Considerable focus is on recovering natural rhythms including breath, pulse, movement, so that the individual may feel centred or able to function from their core. The somatic pathway also emphasizes grounding techniques by which they are ensuring that the person is located fully in their body with awareness down to the tips of their toes. Keleman, cited in Totton, describes this process well:

Grounding means being anchored in our physical
psychic growth processes: expanding, contracting,
charging discharging. Grounding means being rooted
in and partaking of the essence the human animal
function ... separation from the biological ground
results in anguish and despair. (Totton 2003:p.68)

The body pathway is for people who have tried many verbal
pathways and find they cannot really get to the foundations
of blocks to their personal growth and change. The body
pathway has a reputation for taking people to the roots of
the psycho-emotional blocks as it cannot be edited out by
the mind. The client is confronted with the reality of their
emotional trauma that is stored in the bodily cells and which
cannot be avoided, rationalized, denied or avoided because
it simply arises beyond one's conscious mind control. Body
can also provide a means for rapid transformative growth
through artistic processes associated with dance, drama,
gesture, movement, sound, breath and artistic expression.

The hidden costs

There are two general categories of body processes in personal
growth. In the initial category, traumatic material from the
astral is brought to the surface. Holiotropic breathwork is
an example of this approach. In the second approach, the
traumatic material is bypassed and the symptoms experienced
in the body of the astral material are relieved without any
insight into what these astral dynamics might be. Kinesiology
is an example of this approach. Each approach has different
costs and benefits.

Body processes in category one penetrate deeply into mental emotional states of the astral because these traumas are stored in vibrational patterns right down into the bodily cells so can be easily accessed through the body. Repressed, unacknowledged, ignored or sublimated experiences can rise rapidly to the surface of the conscious mind, if entered into by focusing on that part of the body that feels the most tension when speaking about the subject. This technique of focusing was developed by Gendlin (1974) and refined by Tagar (1996), who developed a technique to step into that part of the body to uncover the trauma which he termed the 'enter-exit-behold', which minimizes the client being shocked or flooded by previously repressed traumatic material. Careful skills are need to ensure that not too much material arises at once, and that the client is taught skills and techniques to exit from the traumatic material if they need to, so they do not feel trapped and re-traumatized by it. In addition, if the techniques and processes to integrate the traumatic content into the 'I' are inadequate or absent, then the client can be left feeling flooded and unable to cope with aspects of their day-to-day functioning. In fact, in body-based processes bringing traumatic material to the surface is usually quite easy, the limitations are more in how to handle it when it arises. Tagar's enter-exit-behold technique is a particularly effective way of accessing bodily memory of the trauma by stepping into the bodily place (enter), stepping backwards out of the trauma (exit), then beholding the trauma from a bodily position on the outside of where they trauma was recovered, to gain insight into the trauma and to heal it (beholding) (Sherwood, 2007:p.22).

In category two, the techniques of change bypass the conscious memory of the trauma and techniques are applied to the body through pressure points, muscle testing or the like, to desensitize the body to the aversive response that is causing the trauma to the client. This approach often works very quickly and includes approaches like thought field therapies. Here, the trauma feelings can be avoided but because there is little engagement of the client's consciousness, their 'I', that integrates experiences, then questions of sustainability of the change in the long-term must be considered.

Characteristics of healthy personal growth

1. Promotes the growth of the autonomous 'I'
Category-one body processes have the opportunity to achieve this goal provided they do not flood the client with trauma and cause the client's 'I' or higher mind to excarnate and become even less available to deal with their problems. Category-two processes do not have this characteristic as they are usually practitioner-driven and bypass the 'I'.

2. Emphasizes the client's capacity as initiator of processes
Category-one processes have the possibility of achieving this goal by teaching clients processes and tools that they can apply to their lives on a daily basis. This is not part of category-two processes where the practitioner initiates and primarily directs the process.

3. Provides processes so client can sustain improvements
In both categories there is the potential to provide techniques that the client can use outside of the personal growth training encounter to sustain the acquired improvements. However, this does not always occur and many practitioners rely on regular repeat business rather than working toward teaching the clients tools to self manage. It is essential for sustained

change that there are processes involving repetition to anchor the new behaviour in the bodily cell memory which is done by retraining the etheric or subtle body which controls rhythms in the body.

4. Monitors the client to ensure their 'I' can digest and integrate the experiences

In category one, clients may experience flooding and inadequate tools to process or exit from their experience unless the enter-exit-behold technique is incorporated. In category two, there is often a bypassing of the 'I' in the intervention so as to avoid flooding and retraumatizing but this comprises client ownership of the processes, often leaving the client in a passive rather than active role in their personal growth.

Case study

Katie was thirty-four years old, an attractive single woman with a radiant smile, sensitive eyes and a love of beauty in dress and in nature. She worked as a medical doctor in a country practice and spent most of her leisure time on the beach. She was very committed to personal growth and had undertaken courses, seminars and workshops regularly over the past five years. As part of her quest she had travelled to India, Tibet and Burma. Katie had been a regular pratitioner of meditation for the past two years. She came to therapy following a group personal-growth workshop based on holiotropic breathwork developed by Stanislaw Grof (1975). This is a type of primal regression using a particular style of continuous deep breathing while being exposed to loud evocative music, designed to access the emotional memories in the trauma system (Totton, 2003:p.103).

Katie described the process as happening among a group of about one hundred people who were placed in pairs to work together, taking turns at fulfilling the duties of role A and role B, which meant essentially having turns at going into process while the other person watched over them, then reversing the roles. Person A's instructions were to accompany the client for the whole three hours allocated to the process. This meant sitting beside them when they were in process, accompanying them if they needed to go to the toilet or if they wanted a drink. Person B was to lie on the ground and follow a particular continuous breathing practice while exposed to loud music drawn from indigenous traditions, reminiscent of trance music. The music was so loud that the glass windows of the building shook with the vibrations. Within thirty minutes of breathing and lying on the ground Katie began to have childhood recollections of her family during which she began to remember the quiet repression whenever the father was home from work. Then a feeling of being suffocated arose, like there was a weight lying on the whole of her body and she saw herself for the first time as a five-year-old being raped by her father. He had his hand over her mouth and she felt like she was going to choke for lack of air to breathe. She became panicky and started struggling and trying to scream and started writhing on the ground. She felt as if she were going to die.

Her partner became concerned about her distressed gestures and erratic breathing and struggling and called one of ten support staff who were available if the support person no longer felt able to cope with their partner's behaviours. Two men arrived and asked Katie where she felt the centre of the fear in her body and she pointed to her shoulders and the two men proceeded to apply pressure to her shoulders until she stopped struggling and collapsed with exhaustion. This routine happened three times to Katie during her time as a client, each time throwing up a different sexual abuse scene with her father when she was under the age of eight. On completion of the three-hour process, Katie was exhausted, flooded and in shock and did not know how to integrate this material that had come up through her body into her life. She was fortunate that when it was her turn to watch over her partner; he had a very calm three hours, with no overwhelming traumatic material arising for him so she could continue to focus on her own needs. After completing the weekend, Katie was insightful enough to realize she was in no fit state to return to work on Monday. Not only did she feel unsteady within herself but during the day flashbacks of different episodes of her father sexually abusing her were coming randomly and she felt flooded by the string of memories. Her anxiety level had risen and she noted that she was fearful and experienced feelings of being unable to cope with her life. She had difficulty sleeping, was over-eating junk food and her usual healthy lifestyle had come crashing down around her. She described herself as just wanting to 'sink into a hole in the ground and hide but feeling unable to hide'.

This was Katie's first visit to counselling as she had previously not ever been distressed enough to go to counselling about anything. Using a somatically based holistic counselling process the following steps were undertaken to facilitate Katie's return to a functional life. The first step was to teach her how to exit the traumatic flooding experiences using a simple one-minute technique know as 'Bamboo' (developed by Tagar (1996) and detailed in Sherwood, 2004:p.38).

This was followed by a grounding process to bring her 'I 'back into her body and a very large process of resourcing. This involved facilitating the client to actively access archetypal images and energies that she experienced to be able to protect herself against her fear. The client chose Durga, the Hindu goddess of fierce compassion that can transmute all conditions and is always invincible against the dark forces. Once these processes had adequately restored the client's sense of integrated self or 'I' and the client felt empowered to control the level of exposure to the unpleasant memories of experience, and was ready to work to remove the invasive energetic patterns experienced by the client in her body. The processes were directed by the client's 'I' with the express intention of giving the client tools to manage these processes in her life so that she could experience being in the present moment rather than been drawn unwillingly into past memories.

Summary of the outcomes of healthy and unhealthy personal growth

These will be discussed in light of the case study of Katie

1. I am more present in my daily life
As a result of the holiotropic breathwork workshop, Katie was so flooded with traumatic material stored in her body that she was unable to undertake her day-to-day routines and unable to attend work, drive in a safe manner or complete her daily routine of exercise and self-care. She was not present in her daily life because of the extensive flooding of her 'I' by this previously consciously unexperienced childhood sexual

abuse. At the heart of the problem presented by Katie's experience of the holiotropic breathwork workshop is that her 'I' was not directing the process. It was left to the unconscious bodily experience to be stimulated by breath and sound to throw these patterns up spontaneously. There, Katie experienced herself as a victim of this process, as being flooded by someone else turning on the taps and without her having the skills to know how to turn off the taps because she was drowning in the quantity of material that emerged.

2. I am empowered to shape my destiny

Katie did not experience the workshop as empowering her to initiate what experiences she would choose to work with, or choose how long she would stay in those traumatic experiences, or to increase her sense of being in control of her life. Rather Katie felt thrown into a whirlpool of emotions and bodily sensations that left her feeling like she was going to drown because the feelings were so powerful and her resources to deal with them seemed so negligible. No attention was given to what Katie was physically and etherically able to handle. The excess astral load left her physically depleted, emotionally exhausted and unable to go to her normal workplace because she felt so physically depleted and fragile. Katie has a slender build and this is an indicator that one must be very careful in the amount of traumatic experience such people are exposed to at one time, as slender build usually indicates a thin etheric, while heavily built people usually have a much more robust etheric and are much less affected by emotional material stored in their body.

3. I am increasingly free from reactions

The intensity and vividness of the feelings and images release in the holiotropic breathwork experience brought with it intense feelings of fear, loss, terror, abandonment and, without adequate tools to process these and integrate the experiences into her 'I', Katie was literally trapped in the astral whirlpool of these traumatic imprints which left her feeling abandoned and terrified. Metaphorically but literally, in her body cells she was back to her 5–8-year-old experiences of life being a place of fear and terror over which you have no control. At the end of the workshops she went back to try to live her normal life as the terrified 5–8 year old. This, of course, was detrimental to her overall well-being and functionality in life.

4. I am more fully who I am: 'self-actualization' and 'self-transcendence'

The workshop left Katie feeling less of who she was and unable to continue to work in her profession because of the trauma evoked during it and not adequately processed. Her ability to relate to others declined as she just wanted to disappear and hide down in a hole where no one could find her. This occurred because Katie's memories were significantly overwhelming, and she was not resourced adequately to deal with them prior to the commencement of the breathing, nor was she helped to take control of the experience by being taught basic techniques of how to exit traumatic material when one feels overexposed to it. Traumatic material only triggers helpful growth when it arises at a rate that can be digested by the 'I' and integrated into the higher self's experiences. Then a person may become more of whom they are capable of being rather than less of whom they are capable of being.

The holistic model of personal growth for body, soul and spirit: the consequences

The body is the map of our life's physical, mental and emotional experiences. We walk in the gesture of these frozen experiences. General intentions like 'I want to be peaceful all the time', 'I want to be happy and relaxed', are too vague for the body to work with in a specific context because bodily memories are very specific and stored in specific energy patterns which, as Tagar (1996) indicates, have specific sound resonances. However, once we discover that the body is the non-verbal keeper of all our experiences, the road map of our journeys, then we know that holistic personal development, of whatever nature, must embrace bodily experience. We also become aware that the body is like a sleeping wild tiger and when it is stimulated in such a way as to bring all our experiences to the surface, we must be sure that we can tame the tiger sufficiently for the information that arises to be meaningfully and effectively integrated into our awareness. Getting mauled by the tiger is unskilful and undermines the individual's confidence in managing their personal growth in a holistic and flourishing manner.

Conclusion

The body pathway to personal growth has many strengths in that it can bypass the defence mechanisms that prevent us awakening to our own experience and self-knowledge. In category one though, unless conducted skilfully with the client controlling the process and with good techniques for exiting the experience if the client feels overwhelmed at any stage (bamboo), it can result in flooding the client, profoundly affecting a person's ability to maintain their daily life in some cases.

In category-two experiences, when the client does not need to acquire any consciousness of the underlying problem but experiences immediate relief from the presenting issue in their life, by something that is done to their body by a practitioner, there is more need to review the sustainability of such an approach especially in the long-term. Without the engagement of insight or ' I' presence, we are prone to continue the behaviour that resulted in the presenting issues and rebuild the pattern that has been externally released for us, so that in the long-term we end up back where we began and it becomes a circular pathway.

Although this pathway may be attractive because results can appear to be quick and there appears to be no need to suffer any trauma, in the long-term one must observe carefully to see if the change remains sustainable. Finally, it needs to be pointed out that body-based interventions, where traumatic material arises, have the potential to take the client over threshold one, so that in some cases intense emotions may arise so, for best practice, it is essential to not undertake these interventions without a clear intention of what one wishes to understand or heal in the intervention. In addition, there need to be strong resources that give the vibrational experience of support, strength and courage and have clear knowledge of how to exit material that one experiences as overwhelming and undigestible.

We are now very aware that everything we think and feel ends up in our body cells via the etheric body and that our consciousness or 'I' must permeate every body cell if we are to be present in our lives. We are literally living in an era where our spirit or 'I' must be fully incarnated into our bodies, if we wish to personally develop in sustainable ways. Our real challenge is to be fully present to the present moment in our day-to-day lives. Then we start to create a quality life, a grounded life, fully aware of our bodily responses to the world around us, rather than repressing or evading them through leaving the body. As Thich Naht Hanh insightfully notes that for each one of us: 'The real miracle is not to walk either on water or in the air, but to walk on the earth.'

4. Counselling as pathway

That is all that is holding us together, stories and
compassion.
— Barry Lopez

In the human heart lies the quest to have another
human being listen deeply, carefully, accurately and
empathetically to our story. That is enough to begin our
healing and to promote our personal growth so that the
seeds of our experience may begin to fall on fertile soils.
With many traditional communities and families, people
listen to each others' stories. Now, such support networks
are fragmented and dispersed, more and more people are
finding the need to speak to a counsellor. David Tacey
(2003) goes so far as to suggest that the counsellor for
many people now has the task of helping them connect
with their spirit, a role that was largely the province of the
churches before the secularization of our society. Hence,
counselling is becoming a pathway to reconnecting human
beings to themselves and each other.

Counselling, although once informal, is now a formal
pathway to personal growth and, today, it is essential
for counsellors to be trained, accredited and members of
professional counselling bodies that monitor their members'
standards on a yearly basis throughout their career. While
some counsellors do not meet these standards, most are

unable to access professional insurances. The days of anyone laying claim to the title 'counsellor', without specific training have almost disappeared. This means that there are quality standards within the industry of counselling and professional bodies who work through client grievances. Checking that the counsellor has training and membership of a professional body is always a good start. However, the diversity of counselling modalities, techniques and styles is extensive. Six core distinctions help the client decide which type of counselling they prefer:

1. Length of therapy: Brief therapy which may be completed within 1–3 sessions; mid-term therapy 3–12 sessions; to long-term psychoanalytic therapy, which may extend for 3–10 years depending on presenting issues.

2. Amount of conversation: Verbal therapy, which concentrates on talking through to expressive action therapies which also engage the body on the basis that many feelings cannot be known or even expressed wholly in words.

3. Exposure to your inner trauma: Cognitive Behavioural Therapy (CBT) and associated therapies prefer to focus on external behaviours to manage trauma and increase your defence mechanisms to keep the trauma at bay, while expressive therapies, particularly body-based therapies, work to release the defences so you can experience the trauma and move through it to healing. Even within any one modality of training, the personality and style of the counsellor can considerably influence the type and quality of service delivered.

4. Client-directed versus therapist-directed: The amount of emphasis on the client's autonomy varies in different approaches with the humanistic honouring the client's autonomy to a high degree (Bohart and Tallman, 1998; Rogers, C., 1990) and the behaviouristic far less so (Meichenbaum, 1991).

5. Whole person focus versus focus on mind and behaviour only: Therapists like Pierrakos (1975) focus on the body, etheric or subtle body, mind, heart, spirit relationship, whereas a CBT [see above] therapist will focus primarily on behaviour and mind.

6. Individual versus systems focus: Transpersonal (Welwood, 1983; Rowan, 1990) and family therapists emphasize the role of the individual's connectedness within family, community and other systems (Minuchin, 1974) Most other therapists focus on the individual.

There are many descriptions of the goal of counselling. Victor Frankl (1965) argues that the purpose of our life is to remain optimistic in spite of the tragic triad of pain, guilt and death, and that this quest for meaning is central to the goal of counselling. The humanistic counsellor sees the goal of counselling as enabling the individual to become fully who they are as a person and so manifest their unique gift in their lives and their communities. This is akin to the personal development of a high order or self-actualization. Essentially though, counsellors would be in agreement that the overall aim of counselling is to produce a person who is more able to integrate their life experiences in a skilful way.

The promised benefits

In terms of personal growth, Carl Rogers (1978) articulates the counsellor's role:

> If I can create a relationship characterized on my part
> by a genuineness and transparency in which I am my
> real feelings; by a warm acceptance of and prizing
> of the other person as a separate individual: by a
> sensitive ability to see his world and himself as he sees
> them; then the other individual in the relationship
> will experience and understand aspects of himself
> which previously he has repressed, will find himself
> becoming better integrated, more able to function
> effectively; will become more self-directing, self-
> confident; will become more of a person, more unique
> and more self-expressive, will be more understanding,
> more acceptant of others, will be able to cope with
> the problems of life more adequately and more
> comfortably.

When counselling works well, it should not only help clients to be who they are more fully, but should also help them to discover what is meaningful and to function more skilfully in their day-to-day lives. Their levels of experienced happiness and meaning should rise. Other benefits of counselling include increased compassion towards others as we take responsibility for our own behaviours, rather than project them on to others. Instead of focusing on changing the world and others, counselling enables us to become more content with changing ourselves, so that we first become the change we want to see around us. Counselling thus should open our hearts to connectedness first within ourselves and then to others and in the transforming of our own lives, the ripples should move outwards to transform our families and communities. The change is captured in this beautiful Chinese proverb:

If there is light in the soul,
There will be beauty in the person.
If there is beauty in the person,
There will be harmony in the house.
If there is harmony in the house,
There will be order in the nation.
If there is order in the nation,
There will be peace in the world.

The hidden costs

Counselling as a pathway is full of promise but as a pathway to personal growth is limited not just by the type of counselling training but also by the amount of personal-growth work the counsellor has undertaken themselves. Unless they have walked their talk and continue to do so, then their capacities for supporting others on the personal growth route, will be limited and this, in turn, may restrict or even retard the growth of their clients. In a research paper, 'Client experience in psychotherapy: what Harms and Heals', Sherwood (2001) noted four core harmful experiences (listed below), identified by clients as a result of counselling experiences:

1. Clients experience the counsellor as abandoning them in the face of threatening experiences: Here the clients describe the counsellor as cold, detached and disconnected from their suffering: 'a colourless

person', 'a faceless tool type thing', 'an unknown
quality', who could not be relied upon in a moment
of crisis or fear, much less so if one was feeling
vulnerable or terrified. The counsellor lacks a
supportive presence and increases the client's feelings
of fear and potential fragmentation.

2. Clients experience counsellor acting inauthentically:
   Clients describe their longing for acknowledgment
   of their feelings, not 'some phoney, glib intellectual
   response' or 'smart games' or categorizing them in
   some pre-set boxes that ignores their individuality,
   and which does not allow them to feel valued
   as a person. The relationship between client and
   counsellor is severely constrained by what the client
   experiences as 'better than you' attitude and a
   pretence of 'knowing it all', and treating the client
   like a specimen in a bottle rather than as a living
   breathing human being sharing the same air.

3. Clients feel that they are hijacked by the counsellor's
   personal agenda: Clients' feel the counsellor does not
   help them get control over their problem. 'He was
   pompous ... had a massive ego. I never felt in charge
   of my own treatment ... he was totally in charge.'
   This included being told how to solve the problem
   rather than being led to their own insight, and the
   counsellor filling the session with his own problems
   and issues.

4. Clients experience the therapeutic encounter as
   undermining their esteem and weakening their
   coping skills: Clients felt devalued in the sense of
   feeling dismissed, as though they were unimportant
   and irrelevant to the counsellor or were being

belittled, and this was associated with feeling like
they were being treated like a child instead of an
adult. As a consequence of a counselling relationship
experienced by the client as judgmental and uncaring,
the client's self-esteen may become further fractured.

Other problems that can arise in counselling that have
been recorded include boundary transgression in relation
to sexuality, intimacy and money (Brown, 1999), and
the complications of either ending the sessions too early
or prolonging them too long from the client's viewpoint
(Gibney, 2003). McBride and Tunnecliffe (2002) also identify
a range of legal problems that occur with such breaches of
confidentiality, failure to refer or to follow up appropriately,
and negligent advice. McBride and Tunnecliffe (2002) and
Syme (2003) warn against the hazards of dual relationships
where the counsellor is also a friend, work colleague, relation
or involved in business transactions.

Characteristics of healthy personal growth

1. Promotes the growth of autonomous 'I'
While all counselling modalities would generally agree
that the growth of a healthy integrated autonomous self is
desirable the humanistic, self-psychology, and psychoanalytic
and psychodynamic, as well as holistic counselling would
claim this to be their primary focus. Carl Rogers was the
most vocal exponent of creating the counselling context to
maximize the client's autonomy:

... the therapist is able to let himself go in
understanding this client; that no inner barriers keep

him from sensing what it feels like to be the client
at each moment of the relationship; and that he can
convey something of this empathic understanding
to the client. It means that the therapist has been
comfortable in entering this relationship fully, without
knowing cognitively where it will lead, satisfied with
providing a climate which will permit the client
the utmost freedom to become himself. (Rogers,
1990:p.410)

It is a work of art in progress and counsellors would
emphasize the need for the client to have time to integrate the
parts of themselves and to uncover and unfold aspects of self
not previously owned, acknowledged or explored.

2. Emphasizes the client's capacity as initiator of processes

Again some modalities of therapy, particularly those derived
from the cognitive, behaviourist and psychoanalytic, are
more likely not to have the client initiating the process
but rather taking the patient role whose destiny is largely
directed by the therapist. Again the humanistic tradition
and associated person-centred traditions would emphasize
the importance of the client as the initiator of processes.
Rogers argued:

If the therapy were optimal, intensive as well as
extensive, then it would mean that the therapist has
been able to enter into an intensely personal and
subjective relationship with the client –relating not
as a scientist to an object of study, not as a physician
expecting to diagnose and cure, but as a person to a
person. (Rogers, 1990:p.409)

Many counsellors would see that empowerment in the counselling process is critical for long-term sustainability so that the client leaves with a greater capacity to deal with life's challenges and issues.

3. Provides processes so client can sustain improvements

The effectiveness of counselling in sustaining changes and improvements has been much debated and extensively researched. Essentially, the modality is far less important than the client's relationship with the counsellor, which needs to be characterized by empathy, authenticity and unconditional positive regard to be truly effective (Hariman, 1984). Miller (1999) showed that if there is no experienced improvement by the client in the first three sessions of counselling, then no change will occur in further sessions. It is the client-counsellor relationship that forms the baseline for change and healing.

4. Monitors the client to ensure their 'I' can digest and integrate the experiences

One of the core values in counselling process is to ensure that the client does not remain flooded by traumatic experiences, but is brought to a resolution so they can function in the world without being overwhelmed and unsafe (Jones, 2000). The ethical standards of counselling emphasize the need for this safety although it is not always achieved in practice.

Case study

Jodie was a lithe, delicate woman with wide-set hazel eyes that were striking in their sadness and she dressed in flowing skirts and tops as though she floated rather than walked upon the earth. She was thirty-five when she came to counselling and her wish was to end a five-year relationship with a married man, who was also her counsellor. Jodie had first seen this man as his client, following a traumatic break-up of an earlier relationship that had left her with low self-esteem and feelings of futility and depression. Jodie admitted an instant attraction for her counsellor and that the feeling was mutual and within four weeks he had started taking her out for dinner after the counselling sessions. Within six weeks, they had become lovers.

Jodie initially enjoyed the attention, warmth and closeness that this relationship brought into her then shattered life. She looked forward to her weekly sessions because they would culminate in dinner and sex and time spent with her counsellor/lover. She knew he was married, but as he explained he was only staying until the children grew a bit older, as they were then only two and four years of age. He promised her that once they were school age he would be able to leave and live with her.

Jodie organized her life, her career and her travel around her counsellor/lover and claimed she seemed to get back her joy of life, her energy and will to live again. Jodie continued to see her therapist weekly for the next three years, working on issues of her family system where she experienced being abandoned by her father at ten years of age, when he left to live with another woman and never initiated contact with her again. She also worked on her low self-esteem, her sense of failure in relationships and her bulimia.

Jodie first began to feel unhappy in the relationship when his children reached school age, three years into their relationship, and her lover/counsellor continued to make excuses as to why he could not leave the marriage. Jodie noticed she was feeling increasingly angry, frustrated and grief-stricken. About this time, her lover/counsellor decided that her therapy sessions could now be reduced to monthly sessions, so contact with him declined rapidly and intensified her feelings of despair and frustration. He continued to assure her that he loved her, but was very busy in his expanding practice and that as she was now recovering she did not need so much of his time.

Matters came to a head when she went out to dinner one evening with some friends and caught him in an intimate 'tête à tête' with a very attractive young woman who she knew was not his wife. When she confronted him about it at her next session, he become dismissive and annoyed and informed her that he could live his life how he wished and see who he wished. At his point, Jodie became despairing and decided to give up the relationship for her own peace of mind. However, she found each time she visited him for therapy, she was unable to say no to his sexual advances or requests for intimacy.

Jodie felt like her life was passing her by, and had realized that she was just one of many extramarital relationships in her counsellor's life. Jodie discussed her grief with a friend who suggested a change of counsellor. Jodie had now been in therapy for five years with her lover and her friend pointed out that she was looking and speaking with more distress than before she had begun her therapy five years ago.

When Jodie commenced this holistic therapy, she cancelled any future appointments with her previous counsellor/lover and had not heard from him for six weeks. However, she admitted she was longing for a phone call from him, and would not be able to say no, even though she knew that it was in her interests to move on from the relationship. Jodie had a number of issues to clear before she was able to speak up to her ex-lover and resist his advances. These included clearing the sense of betrayal and broken trust, nurturing her own abandoned ten-year-old child that was projecting the lost father onto the ex-lover, rebuilding her sense of self-esteem and working to establish boundaries. Like many women caught in these situations with a counselling or medical professional, she chose not to report his behaviour to his professional association as she just wanted to move on and rebuild her life.

Summary of the outcomes of healthy and unhealthy personal growth

1. I am more present in my daily life

The case study illustrates the compromising effect on the client's well-being of crossing professional boundaries. Initially the client's feelings of abandonment were lifted and she experienced herself as being more present to her life, but once the reality of the situation began to manifest in the broken promises and observation of other lovers, Jodie became less present to he life and experienced sinking more and more into depression.

2. I am empowered to shape my destiny

Boundary violations by practitioners make the client more vulnerable and needy and dependent on the counsellor/ lover for meaning and direction in their life. Jodie was an unhappy example of giving up her independence and shaping her life around her lover who was, in reality, using her good will for his convenient satisfaction. There was no evidence that despite the hundreds of sessions that Jodie had completed with her lover/ex-counsellor, that she was more empowered or more able to shape her destiny than prior to commencing therapy with him. She appeared very dependent and so deeply disempowered that she was having difficulty saying no to a relationship with her ex-counsellor, even when she realized it was deeply exploitative.

3. I am increasingly free from reactions

Jodie's levels of anger, fear, abandonment, frustration and vulnerability although initially reducing, rose sharply in the last two years of the relationship and were very high when she arrived at holistic counselling. This is clear evidence of the helpfulness of the many sessions completed, which were clearly hijacked by the counsellor's personal agenda towards the client, for his own self-interests rather than her therapeutic interests. Brown (1999) also describes candidly how and why a needy therapist uses a client to meet his emotional needs.

4. I am more fully who I am: 'self-actualization' and 'self-transcendence'

This clearly did not occur in Jodie's case of practitioner-boundary violation. On the contrary, Jodie's personal and social life became closed down and restricted to limited times when her lover was available. Her sense of self remained vulnerable and dependent on his approval and fragmented easily when it became obvious to her, that he was no longer seriously interested in her. Self-actualization and self-transcendence occurs primarily in the transpersonal model of therapy, as well as some body-based models including core energetics. In the fourfold model, it is the connection with the archetypes in the transpersonal that gives the client the resources of courage and strength to move through what otherwise can be experienced as overwhelming or insurmountable personal obstacle in the client's life. Part of freeing Jodie and strengthening her, was to work with her to find an archetypal resource that was meaningful to her and would give her a sense of connectedness. She chose to work with Maat, the Eypgtian goddess of justice, as well as choosing to buy a pet dog to provide immediate warmth, love and comfort.

The holistic model of personal growth for body, soul and spirit: the consequences

There is great diversity among the different modalities of counselling so that the impacts on the clients may vary considerably, particularly in light of a holistic model of personal growth. It is like a forest of many different species, each with something different to offer but all providing some basic shelter. The depth of the roots of each tree and the span of its branches will vary depending on the theoretical perspective of the counselling practitioner. Some counselling modalities focus on the thinking of the client, others on the willing or behaviours, and some more on the feelings. The body-based approaches try to integrate these levels in the body. Core energetics and the holistic counselling models try to integrate thinking, willing and feeling to produce a balanced human being that is integrated energetically into a harmonious fit with the energy systems around him (Pierrakos, 1987:p.19).

At the heart of the process is recovering the feeling that life is working through the astrality to reduce sympathies and antipathies that drive reactive patterns and cause us to blame others for our misery. These projections melt away when we free ourselves in the counselling process so that we no longer need to be the victim of those around us, but can rise up empowered and set sail on the oceans of life, piloting our own boat with skilfulness, and with satisfaction.

Conclusion

The client-counsellor relationship is the central defining quality in the effectiveness of the interaction, which is summarized beautifully by Carl Rogers:

> In the therapeutic relationship some of the most
> compelling subjective experiences are those in which
> the client feels within himself the power of naked
> choice. He is free to become himself or to hide behind
> a façade. (Rogers, 1990:p.417)

The client must be encouraged to make choices from the position of authenticity which then supports the strengthening of the client's insight or the 'I'. Then, as the astral reactions of anger, fear grief and loss are cleared, the client can begin to speak up clearly for who they are or are becoming. It is a wonderful and awesome process of personal growth at its best, which brings healthy growth and skilful change into the client's life. It is the client, exerting their own power, their own insight, that drives the change process, as they unfurl their wings to manifest their fullness. It is captured poetically in this beautiful image of the butterfly: 'Change is a whirlwind and you are the butterfly whose wings make it happen' (Changeling. www.faery.shaman.co.uk)

5. Guru as pathway

It is unwise to be too sure of one's own wisdom. It is healthy to be reminded that the strongest might weaken and the wisest might err.
— Gandhi

The word guru is made of two syllables of which 'gu' means the darkness and 'ru' the one who dispels, according to Swami Satchidananda (1977:p.1), who goes on to define the guru as the 'one who helps you in realizing your own spirit by removing the ignorance which veils it.' However, as Swami Yogananda in his famous work, Autobiography of a Yogi, emphasizes, external gurus should only be regarded as a pathway to awaken a person to the guru within their own consciousness, the place of true awakening, which can direct their lives from the highest consciousness of insight and wisdom. The guru as pathway to awakening and enlightenment has been adopted in western capitalist countries by elevating charismatic teachers, often eastern, to positions of spiritual leadership, resulting in a devotee following their directions and imitating their behaviour. The list is long: the Divine Light Mission and Radhasoami, The Orange People and Rajneesh, the Hari Krishnas and Swami Prabhupada, the devotees of Sai Baba, Swamiji, Maharishi, Master Choa Kok Su, Mother Mary, to name a few. Some gurus like Rajneesh made the commodification and commercialization of their charisma their focus and became exceedingly wealthy at the hands of western followers (Urban, 2002). In the past twenty years the guru movement has been secularized and mobilized to support the growth of the corporate world. Corporate gurus like Anthony Robbins, are also very wealthy. In the self-help personal-growth industry, gurus like John Gray, Suze Orman, Shirley MacLaine, Doreen Virtue, Brandon Bays, all have wealth, devotees, status and influence.

Whether secular, spiritual, or a mixture, the term guru defines people who possess charisma. Weber (1968) denied charisma as the presence of leaders who have the qualities of magnetism, power, charm and personal authority independent of the status of office or rank. Charismatic leaders do not exist in a vacuum but rather arise in situations where people's anxiety and dispiritedness call for leadership that can transcend the boredom or futility of everyday routine and provide meaning, enthusiasm and purpose to otherwise mundane existences. The charismatic leader brings vision, hope and enthusiasm to the followers who are often already educated and affluent but seeking a broader horizon for their lives. Katz (1999) illustrates this phenomenon with the rise of the Internet gurus such as Rheingold, Barlow, Dyson, Kelly, Gates and Turkle who have opened vision to the vast horizons of cyberspace. Clark and Salaman (1996) see the management guru as succeeding in revitalizing the emotional and symbolic aspects of an organization by identifying them and imbuing them with a power that enthuses and meaningfully touches the lives and hearts of employees. Gurus provide medicine for the human soul when its quest to live falters or ails because it has lost its vision and purpose. La Barre (1980) argues insightfully that the unconscious masses search for a guru and ascribe to them the power to define their vision and purpose and articulate a way through their unmet needs for meaning.

The guru voices the truth in their experience that they have not yet named but feel to be omnipresent in their lives. They offer the promise of transcendence beyond people's small lives, a connectedness to a vision that is vast and great and which can frame their lives meaningfully. McIlwain (2006) notes accurately that the appeal comes from 'the mesh of its promise with a person's often unspoken or unacknowledged longings.'

The promised benefits

The guru offers his followers freedom from fear of uncertainty and powerlessness, an insightful new knowledge base, explanations to account for the challenges in their experience, and the promise of a meaningful way forward in their lives. One's own inner deficits, lack of motivation and enthusiasm for life are compensated by the presence of the guru who meets these needs. The guru offers a way through a lifestyle rut, relief from inner boredom and sterility by offering freshness, change, invigoration and renewed stamina for life. This is very attractive in a society that is increasingly defunct of meaning and motivation beyond materialism. The secular gurus turn even the pursuit of materialism into a motivational icon by emphasizing the collective national consciousness or symbols of personal meaning which are packaged within product sales (Katz, 1999). Dawson (2006:pp.11f) notes that key to the successful charismatic leader is an intense relationship with his followers that is characterized by five emotionally satisfying rewards for the followers, which are:

1. relief from the tension of failing to live up to an ego-ideal as described by Freud in the sense of the gap between our self-expectations and our self-behaviour;

2. fulfilment of an ego-ideal by the leader which relieves the followers of the feelings of their own failure;

3. projection onto the leader of success, which brings about a state of euphoria that intensifies and elevates the leader to a profound position in the followers' psyche;

4. recognition of the leader's power and value reinforces the followers' commitment to the leader and the rightness of their choice;

5. well-being of the individual devotee is inextricably woven with the leader who now holds the followers' sense of self-worth and who promotes and enlarges the follower's sense of perceived self-value.

The charismatic leader provides rituals, processes and rites, which enrich mundane experiences of followers and which enshrine in their hearts a more meaningful purpose to life (Dawson, 2006).

The hidden costs

Too often, the followers develop a lifestyle of dependency upon the guru who inspires, motivates and holds the vision that gives their lives meaning and purpose, without the follower actually integrating this into their 'I' through their own efforts. Gurus can become an illusionary shortcut to cultivating one's own place of insight and self-awareness and to developing one's own autonomy through integrating one's own experiences. They are then elevated to the position of superior wisdom, and their 'I' displaces the client's own 'I', which can result in a slavish following of the guru's directions even when common sense predicts otherwise, and an unquestioning acceptance of even exploitative demands from the guru. The neediness of the followers elevate the guru to a position of superiority which can easily bring out narcissistic tendencies in the guru. This occurs when the guru becomes pre-occupied in accumulating excessive wealth because they are so superior to other people, or demanding compliance to rules and behaviour from their followers that they do not comply with themselves. Potentially, this can lead to the exploitation of the followers in one or more respects because they are dependent on the guru's love, approval, acceptance and direction in their lives. Essentially, the guru has taken over the position of the follower's 'I' to varying degrees, and is now running the follower's life. The followers have attributed to him 'charisma' which, Weber (1968) notes, encompasses the perception of the guru as superhuman, supernatural or bearing exceptional powers or qualities which the followers feel unable to access in themselves. This leaves the followers vulnerable to the ethical behaviour of the guru, which does not always maintain its original clarity and benevolence, given the human propensity to experience power as corrupting. This is particularly the case when the guru has not completely cleared their own astrally driven needs and desires. The guru then uses their superior position of power to extract money, sex, gifts, or the like from his followers, who are left feeling used, betrayed, exploited and often discarded. In the worst scenarios, the misuse of charismatic authority has even led some people to commit acts of violence towards themselves, their family or others (Dawson, 2006).

The quality of the charismatic bond determines whether the outcome will be benign or destructive. The more authoritarian and narcissistic the charismatic guru, the greater the likelihood that emotional, mental, or even physical violence may occur among the devotees. Also, the more authoritarian the guru, the more trauma there is when leaving or defecting. Wright (1989) noted that 42% of his sample leaving a guru did so secretly, and 40% experienced dislocation from their lives. Samways (1994:p.670) also criticizes many of the recruitment processes used by gurus in the personal-growth industry, which she claims embrace vague and misleading advertisements, and invitations to obscure events which have hidden agendas. Such an illustration is the landmark forum which sometimes uses graduation events. They may ask the graduates to bring along friends to their graduation. The friends think they are celebration events only to find that such an occasion is really the thin veneer of a recruitment session with techniques such as demanding that guests give good reasons as to why they will not enrol in one of their personal-growth seminars, before leaving the ceremony.

Characteristics of healthy personal growth

1. Promotes the growth of autonomous 'I'
Gurus have a long history of not promoting the growth of the 'autonomous' 'I' in their followers despite publicity and assertions to the contrary. Certainly, people who have been under the influence of a particular guru, whether secular, spiritual or a mix, too often take on the world-view of that guru which involves speaking, dressing and behaving in ways that meet the guru's prescribed advice. People not

under the influence of the guru when meeting the followers of a particular guru, often experience conversations with them as though one is speaking to a tape-recorded message or a standard hype message that is disconnected from the individual's unique 'I'. It is as though the guru's 'I' stands in the place of it. Unfortunately, once a convert to a particular guru, it is difficult to see how one's own 'I' has disappeared into the guru-speak of the 'in group'. However, it is very obvious to people not belonging to the group that the individuality of a friend or colleague is fast disappearing into 'group-speak' and group behaviour. This retards the growth of the autonomous 'I', particularly if the individual is seduced by the charisma and the message for a prolonged period of time.

2. Emphasizes the client's capacity as initiator of processes

Traditionally, gurus provide a hierarchy that followers need to climb to get to positions of being able to initiate processes. Followers at the bottom of the hierarchy may have little power to initiate while those at the top of the hierarchy, and close to the guru, may have considerable power to initiate within the frameworks of meaning and control established by the guru. In fact, sometimes senior power holders actually take over the control of followers, and the guru becomes a figurehead or, at worst, a puppet, poorly informed of the behaviours of the controlling members in the senior hierarchy. Status intimidation prevents other people from challenging healthy practices and creates the I/them split, and leaves those lowest in the hierarchy with very low levels of autonomy and ownership of the processes they undertake.

3. Provides processes so client can sustain improvements

Gurus can provide processes and pathways to sustain personal improvements and often they are extremely prescribed behaviours and ideas around how this sustainability can be reached. The key question in terms of the quest for self, is whether they impart tools and processes that are self-administering in the long-term, and not dependent on the guru. In the former case, such guru advice may be very helpful on the pathway to one's own empowerment. It is excellent to receive tips about how to navigate certain difficult road conditions for example, by someone who is already familiar with the road terrain. In the latter case, the guru constricts the client's growth and acquisition of new skills because the client remains dependent upon the guru for the same services repeatedly which will limit the growth of their own autonomous self. The distinction is very important and is like the old story: that while it is good to provide food for a hungry person, it is better to teach then how to fish, so that in the long-term they are independent of the need for ongoing support.

4. Monitors the client to ensure their 'I' can digest and integrate the experiences

This monitoring of the follower or client may occur but it is focused on the guru's agenda and very often the real needs of the clients' agenda are overlooked. Integration is often not based accurately on the devotees' 'I' and rather the guru's 'I' is superimposed. In the long-term this can result in breakdowns, and break-outs or defections by seemingly committed followers. This is why some people who become disillusioned with their guru, can caste off the accoutrements quite quickly because it was superimposed and superficial. People whose deep unmet needs are fulfilled by the guru's message have much greater difficulty moving away and letting go.

Case study

Sarah was an American marketing executive and a very intelligent woman in her early fifties. She had a seventeen-year-old daughter with whom she lived. Sarah had raised the daughter by herself from when the child was one year's old. Sarah's own father had died when she was one year's old, and her mother had remarried a man who rejected her and Sarah had left home at fourteen years of age to live with friends. Her first boyfriend had died in a car accident, her second boyfriend, the father of her child, had been killed while hiking overseas and her best friend had died suddenly of a brain tumour. Sarah though, had a quiet courage and determination to survive and had worked hard to support herself and her daughter as a sole parent, having obtained a degree in marketing, and worked as a successful marketing manager in a corporate company in the United States.

Sarah described herself as a spiritual person, very conscious of the higher nature of herself and those around her. She had been a student of Swamiji and experienced the light as within herself and within other people. She was very committed to personal growth and followed daily meditation practices to cultivate her awareness of self and others. For three years she had been part of a group of people following a spiritual teacher called Ted, who claimed to be an esoteric teacher of the spiritual pathway to personal growth and fulfilment. Ted was, as Sarah explained, very charismatic and an excellent teacher of pathways to claim one's inner strength and truth. Sarah was not easily taken in by spiritual teachers but liked Ted and believed that his emphasis on his students taking responsibility for their own inner pathway and cultivating their own power within themselves was very commendable. She had seen many of her friends go down the Rajneesh pathway, and was quietly concerned at how they allowed themselves to be exploited financially, sexually and personally. Ted was different because he gave the individual the responsibility for their personal growth and only taught techniques and processes that would facilitate the individual to develop their fullness. Ted ran a clean show and warned about the hazards of using drugs as a process to personal growth and established clear boundaries prohibiting sex with his followers. It looked like Ted had read all the books on how the charismatic leader can go wrong, and Ted was going to avoid these pitfalls. Weekly meetings occurred with Ted leading the group, which included Sarah's teenage daughter, and teaching them a range of useful exercises for inner awakening.

Sarah arrived for counselling and began weeping and visibly shaking from time to time with her distress. She had discovered that her seventeen-year-old daughter, who she thought was not sexually active, was pregnant by an unknown father; at least, her daughter refused to name the father. Sarah was beside herself with concern because of what she regarded as her daughter's emotional immaturity and financial and emotional dependence upon her. Sarah confided that after considerable pressure, leading questions and detective work her daughter had finally admitted that Ted was the father. Sarah reeled in shock, horror and disbelief and spoke of feeling betrayed to the depths of her heart by Ted, who she had always honoured as teaching both her and her daughter high moral standards by which to live life.

As the story unravelled, it came to light that Ted had taken her daughter to his home one evening to a party where sex and drugs were on the menu. The result of her unprotected sexual activity was pregnancy. When Sarah confronted Ted about his use of drugs and random unprotected sex with her daughter, both standards of which he disapproved, Ted remained unapologetic and was concerned that the matter be concealed from the other followers, because it would undermine his reputation and leadership in the group. He did not want the child, did not want to support her daughter through, or after, the pregnancy, and rationalized that it was a one-off event and best forgotten.

Sarah was despairing because at that moment she knew she was utterly alone with the problem and her confidence and trust in this person had been betrayed. She was left to work out with her depressed daughter how to support her through the unwanted pregnancy and the disowning father. Sarah says that at that point in time she realized she had lost her friend, teacher, confidant, motivator, inspirer and that she would have to survive the situation alone and support her daughter who was also emotionally fragmented and shattered, and who had genuinely believed that Ted had loved her and now had to deal with her abandonment and her pregnancy, with very few resources or skills. Sarah courageously reclaimed herself, working with betrayal, then her sense of grief and loss, abandonment, invasion and aloneness. She worked to fulfil her unmet needs that she had been projecting upon Ted and with strength and commitment found strong foundations on which to work through the difficult months that lay ahead for herself and her daughter.

Ted is a case study of someone who assumes the guru position because they have the charisma to do so and because they can meet their followers' needs, but who have not cleared their own astral patterns of aversions and desires which leaves them vulnerable to falling from the pedestal of guruhood through their own crumbling feet of clay. The problem is when gurus fall they usually land on some of their followers, causing psychological and other types of damage. For Sarah and her daughter, Ted represented the present caring male and they were vulnerable to project this on to him because of all the absent men in their experience. Somewhere, he had filled up the great empty chasms in their lives left by the men who had abandoned them. This, of course, made the betrayal of trust more devastating for both Sarah and her daughter as Sarah realized how alone and empty she really felt.

Summary of the outcomes of healthy and unhealthy personal growth

1. I am more present in my daily life
Sarah would claim that many of the techniques that Ted taught in his group were beneficial to her, helping her manage her daily life more skilfully and become more confident and present to her life. She would also say though that the shock of his betrayal, by someone so close to her daughter, forced her to seek to become more present to her daily life and to cope with this challenging life change with her daughter.

2. I am empowered to shape my destiny
Sarah did experience some empowerment over the years to direct her life destiny through the teachings of Ted, but at an emotional, psychological level did not realize how vulnerable and dependent she had become on Ted for support, advice and goodwill in her day-to-day life. Her emotional collapse and feelings of helplessness and vulnerability after the betrayal confronted her with the subtle degree of dependency she had built up around Ted, her teacher and guru. Such

a psychological collapse is typical of the more subtle type of guruship where the guru does not exercise behavioural control directly over the follower's life, but psychologically has a major, if not directing, place in the follower's soul life. The problem with the guru approach to personal growth is that too often the guru, rather than becoming a stimulus for the person to develop their own 'I' or underdeveloped qualities so that they become more self-governing, becomes the followers' 'I' and directs their lives in subtle ways. The needy follower projects their unmet needs and weakness onto the guru to fill the gap in their own sense of self. This results in a dependency in the longer term upon the guru and/or the community of followers, and a weakening of the autonomous self.

3. I am increasingly free from reactions

Sarah did initially experience increasing insight through Ted's teaching because he was very impressive philosophically. Ted was supportive, giving advice and teaching Sarah in a way that she experienced as helpful because she then experienced less reactive feelings like fear. However, as soon as Ted challenged her life values and daughter, through his behaviour, then the foundations of the relationship proved fragile and her reactions of fear, anger, abandonment and loss came to the surface and were enlarged as a result of the unsatisfactory end to her relationship with her guru. One might suggest that this pathway, in which the follower initially feels less reactive is usually common, until some experience emerges that cannot be solved by the guru relationship, and then the repressed or sublimated reactions emerge even more strongly than before meeting the guru. The person is then left more vulnerable and more exposed to their own fragility than before commencing the relationship with the guru.

In addition, observing the client's body to ascertain the

balance between the astral breakdown processes and the etheric, physical building-up processes is not often part of they way gurus function. They often give out a message which is defined somewhere as universal for a particular group, without serious attention to individual differences in physical constitution. The Landmark Forum is an example of a personal-growth process which does not always adequately understand the catabolic, anabolic relationship. Many individuals, particularly those who are robust physically, flourish in the mental, emotional and physical challenges provided by the Landmark Forum. However, some individuals whose catabolic processes already well exceed their anabolic processes and who are only just holding their lives together by a thread, attend Landmark and breakdown into flooding and personal disorganization and are less able to cope with their day-to-day lives, than prior to attending the forum. Not only do they feel more emotionally vulnerable and fragile but physically they also feel exhausted and less able to cope with the daily demands of their lives.

4. I am more fully who I am: 'self-actualization' and 'self-transcendence'

The relationship with the guru may initially result in a widening of relationships with a new community of people who are part of the 'in group' but usually, over time, this proves to be constricting, as relationships with people not part of the in group are likely to radically diminish. Some parts of the guru's message can, in many cases, encourage the person to develop parts of themselves previously hidden or repressed, but the difficulty is when parts of who they are must be repressed, denied or avoided because they are not congruent with the ethos, values or messages propounded by the guru and accepted by the in-group.

The holistic model of personal growth for body, soul and spirit: Consequences

The guru process of personal growth usually relies upon the guru's passion, motivation or vision to define the change process and to direct and originate it. Depending on the individual, some people will own the process deeply and make it their own through conscious acts of their own willing, whereas other people will go along with it superficially but later detach from it easily because it is not integrated into their own will. Personal growth that has long-term sustainability does require the individual to invest their own will deeply in the deeds that they undertake. In addition, the best gurus not only inspire their followers' deeds but also encourage them to connect to their feeling life, so that their deeds are infused with compassion and their thoughts are infused with warmth and ethical foundations. This then will result in personal growth that is respectful of the individual and those that the individual encounters.

Conclusion

The guru pathway can be powerful and inspirational for many people as it can offer movement from positions of personal immobility and meaningless, and can help motivate people to move onto the next step of their growth process. However, individuals are prone to project their unmet needs onto the guru and become dependent upon them to direct their well-being and happiness. They allow them to take over the 'I' position within their lives. This guru-disciple relationship can become dysfunctional when the guru falls apart or shows feet of clay or, worse, starts to use his elevated position in the place of the disciple's 'I' to direct the disciple's actions so that they become destructive or exploitative to the disciple. They may be damaged psychologically and find it difficult to regather themselves and to recover their own 'I', their self-esteem and self-integration. Swami Satchidananda, reflecting on the difficulties of choosing a guru who is likely to be helpful on the spiritual pathway, suggests three outcomes which provide the litmus tests for skilful gurus:

1. Does the guru practise what he preaches? Does his own behaviour follow his advice to his disciples?

2. What are the results of the guru's behaviour and teachings upon the lives of his followers? Do they demonstrate skilful changes in their lives as a result of contact with the guru?

3. Does the guru inspire the followers with confidence that they will be guided effectively for their best benefit and well-being?

(Swami Satchidananda, 1979:pp.34–36)

Those who choose to walk the guru pathway are vulnerable to all the strengths and weaknesses of their guru. The threats of domination, delusion and exploitation can have high costs for the aspirant whose guru is driven by desires for wealth, power and status. In contrast, security, wisdom and rapid personal growth are the reward for the disciple of the truly enlightened guru who has freed himself first from all aversions and desires, all cravings for power and who has developed the compassionate mind which is the most solid foundation for all knowledge and wisdom.

6. Psychics as pathway

I like to think of psychic energy as akin to radio
waves. Even without the radio on, the air is filled with
invisible signals from countless radio stations operating
on their various frequencies. All you have to do to
receive them is to flick the radio on and tune the dial.
— John Edward

Attend any personal-growth fair, trade festival or expo and
observe the steady stream of clients wending their way to
join the queues waiting for the psychics. Often attired in
dramatic colourful, cosmic-patterned or 'in-role' clothing,
and complete with crystal balls, the psychics command many
people's attention and willingness to pay substantial amounts
of money for a consultation. Psychics have been variously
defined from charlatans to prophets and are believed by
many clients to have powers to see into the past, solve
current problems and predict the future. They are attributed
by clients with extra-sensory perception, that is, the capacity
to see things in the past, present or future unknown to the
clients, and which the client feels unable to access using their
own powers of perception. Psychics may be born with these
powers, inheriting them from descendents who possessed
them, or they may have had a severe or life-threatening
experience and their psychic abilities arise out of the suffering
(www.psychic.com).

Despite the paucity of scientific research validating the accuracy of the psychic process and an increasing body of research (Wiseman & West, 1996) demonstrating that the process is inaccurate and without validity, its popularity in our culture is increasing. Certainly, as Lyons and Truzzi (1991) indicate it is very difficult to measure scientifically and a number of psychics continue to be consulted by police because they can provide information to facilitate some criminal investigations (Nickell, 1994). Critical evaluation of psychics in police work though remains controversial and there is much debate about the accuracy of statements such 'the person will be found in a body of water', which has a range of interpretations (Reiser et al., 1979). Given that we live in a culture dominated by the scientific and material ethos why then are psychics currently one of the most popular personal-growth pathways?

Essentially, people who come to psychics have needs that cannot be met by science and technology. Zygmut (1972) noted that people choose one pathway rather than another because they experience their problems to be more meaningfully addressed in the chosen pathway. Moreover, a series of sociologists including Lasch (1979), Bell (1976) and Cock (1979) noted that when a culture loses its ethics, meaning and community ethos, then there is a trend by some people to feel vulnerable, uncertain and victims, while other people feel overly powerful and able to provide leadership to the vulnerable. These two responses are like the hooks and clasps in Velcro. Essentially, psychics offer solutions to people feeling uncertain, vulnerable, unhappy and, in some ways, directionless and disempowered. They provide the vision and direction for these people's lives that has been lost in our secular, materialistic society. Interestingly, they are listed in telephone directories with 'hot lines' not far away from other emergency services. If the emotional pain, emptiness or abandonment in the present moment feels unbearable, and one has no tools to transform them into hope, optimism and joy or meaning, then the psychic can offer immediate relief. Whether the psychic's predications transpire is often a secondary consequence. Their immediate role is often to provide a new perspective on the client's experience that promises hope, and can arouse new expectations and provide some faith that there is a light at the end of the tunnel that they currently find themselves trapped within. Psychics at their best generate hope and purpose, provide a lamp in the darkness and a map guiding the future of someone's life, which can otherwise feel so random for some people.

The promised benefits

From the client's point of view the benefits vary but include feeling relief from uncertainty and aloneness as evidenced by psychic advertisements specializing in relationship advice: past, present and future. In addition, some clients experience it as a quick way to solve problems and make difficult decisions. Painful traumas can be endured if the psychic can predict a positive outcome in the future or explain past reasons for the trauma. Essentially, psychics can create, manage, re-frame and dissolve meaning in client's lives, particularly in relation to the client's experiential, feeling lives for which science has little to offer. As one very intelligent young woman said to me: 'Science is interesting and useful but it doesn't make one happy.' Materialism, the handmaiden of science, has also failed to deliver consistent and sustainable happiness to people. Layard (2005:p.33) cites data confirming that after income levels reach $20,000 per head in a country, additional income is not associated with extra happiness. Instead, the key predictors of happiness are your inner life as reflected in your state of mind, your social relationships, your feelings of trust in other people, and avoidance of losses (Layard, 2005:pp.225–27). The search for happiness has gone elsewhere: recreational drugs, religious revivals, gurus, guides, counsellors, life coaches and psychics.

The hidden costs

The psychic approach to personal growth is other-directed not self-directed so it does not support the growth of autonomy within the client, nor encourage self- responsibility or self-motivation. It is too easy to become habitually dependent on a psychic and to run one's life from this position of dependency. The validity of the prediction can be minimized by clients psychologically, provided the psychic offers positive affirming predictions that temporarily assuage the client's need for security and happiness. However, one unfortunate implication is that clients may fail to take action to change something critical in their lives because they are waiting for the predicted event to happen, or they may take action to change something prematurely because of a psychic prediction. An example is a person who sold her house and all her possessions and travelled over 3,000 kilometres to a place where the psychic predicted she would find her 'soul mate'. After waiting there for over twelve months she became increasingly depressed as no such person appeared. In her depression, she stopped working, developed an eating disorder and began to seek a way out through recreational drugs. She felt cheated, disheartened and suicidal in her despair and aloneness, convinced that she would never find true love and that only drugs could solve the pain. Also, some less skilful psychics will share predictions with the client that are liable to increase the client's feelings of weakness, insecurity and hopelessness by predicting dire or difficult events arising in the client's life, such as illness, loss of home, break-up of family or death of loved ones. This can erode a client's already fragile sense of self and their capacity to originate their life direction, and they can become fatalistic and deterministic, which ends in the client becoming the disempowered victim. This is the opposite outcome to personal growth, which should result in empowering a person to take control of their lives to become more fully who they wish to be.

There appear to be no accredited professional standards that psychics need to conform to, so one can expect their skills to be highly variable and encompass the good, the bad and the ugly. There is no recourse to checking out their competencies except by personal experience or hearsay, and in these situations the client is in a very vulnerable position and open to a rollercoaster of experience with different psychics.

Characteristics of healthy personal growth

1. Promotes the growth of autonomous 'I'
It is clear that the psychic relationship to the client is not one that develops the autonomous 'I' but rather it encourages other dependency and weakens the self-originating 'I'. This undermines the healthy psychological growth of the integrated self with the client being the originator of deeds in their own lives. However, when the client's 'I' is crumbling,

an empathetic psychic might hold a safe space for the client to gather the pieces of themselves back to themselves.

2. Emphasizes the client's capacity as initiator of processes

The client does not initiate the process of uncovering their destiny but rather relies on the psychic to initiate and communicate the information that the psychic chooses to communicate. This creates considerable dependency upon the psychic and the client abandons their role as the initiator of their own personal growth that is so critical to healthy psychological growth. Ideally, the client needs to learn their own skills to access their own inner life and direction, rather than prematurely crossing the first threshold with the assistance of the psychic. The crossing of the first threshold takes time to develop the inner resources of courage and strength and to develop appropriate tools to integrate all of one's self and experience. However, the longer time period taken to learn to cross one's own threshold, gives the client greater control over the process and greater reliability in the authenticity of uncovering one's own experience.

3. Provides processes so client can sustain improvements

Psychics rely upon repeat business as it is not a process that is imparted to clients to enable them to initiate and sustain changes and improvements in their lives. Rather the client tends to rely upon the psychic for the next, and the next prediction that can improve their lives. For some clients, visiting a psychic is just for fun as they have a well developed sense of self, but for vulnerable clients with weak senses of self, they may become addicted to psychics and experience fear if they feel unable to contact them, and may live their life by their psychic's predictions.

4. Monitors the client to ensure their 'I' can digest and integrate the experiences

While sensitive and empathetic psychics no doubt monitor the client's ability to digest information and so only provide an edited amount, many psychics are demonstrably unaware of some clients' inability to deal with certain troublesome information and the consequences on the clients' life of such indigestible information. They give the client information because they have it and they can, and they have no training to assess its corroding effect upon the clients' self, or they way it can compound issues of shame, guilt, self-judgement, powerlessness already resonant within the client. The case study below illustrates this problem in detail.

Case study

Anna arrived at counselling clearly very agitated and very red. From head to toe she was covered with red blotches that were ugly and angry. She was visibly pregnant, and she had obviously been crying for a long time because her eyes were red rimmed to match her skin. Anna was twenty-five years old, a nurse from Argentina who had no children, despite her intention to do so and having been married for five years. She was not a confident person. Through the tears Anna explained that she and her husband desperately wanted a child. Finally, she had become pregnant and they were delighted, but five and a half months into the pregnant, she began to haemorrhage and the doctor feared she may lose the baby. Heartbroken at the thought, she began to discuss her distress with a close friend who recommended she seek help from a psychic. The psychic was well known had a large client group, and her reputation for accuracy and reliability was highly esteemed.

The psychic was a mature woman in her forties who ran a very busy and popular psychic practice that was attended by dozens of men and women wanting predictions and insight into their lives and their problems. Her friend had her speak to several people who had had personal experience of this psychic and who believed their lives had greatly benefited from their sessions with her. Anna visited the psychic about two days after the doctor's news, in the midst of her fear and grief about the potential of losing her child. What Anna remembers vividly from her one-hour encounter with the psychic was the psychic explaining to her that as Anna had killed a child deliberately in a previous life, the karmic consequence was the probable loss of this child she was carrying. She had demonstrated that she was an unworthy, unloving mother in a previous life and this was the karmic consequences of that behaviour.

Anna says she was rendered speechless and left the room feeling despairing. The psychic may have said other things to Anna, but this is all that she could recall. Within forty-eight hours after visiting the psychic, Anna awoke with her body covered with this ugly, red itchy rash which was particularly fierce around her throat. Anna's bodily gestures alternated between fear and repressed anger. Anna had two wishes or intentions that she wished to pursue in the counselling sessions:

1. to stop the rash itching and to clear it;
2. to eliminate the fear that she would lose her baby.

The first wish was accomplished by having Anna step into her body and through a series of questions, gesture and sounds and drawings, identify what emotions were contained within the rash which were, predictably, imploded anger, feeling judged and the inability to speak up. After releasing the anger, Anna identified her feeling of guilt underlying it which was of parental judgment and condemnation. The energetic force of the judge's voice in her body was removed and she resourced forgiveness by her choosing to connect with Mother Mary and receive through sound, gesture, movement and visualizing the loving acceptance of this archetype.

The next day, when Anna returned for her second session, the rash had disappeared, coincidentally with the session or otherwise. Anna was delighted. We then followed up with a fear sequence about losing the baby. Here we found her own shame at not 'being good enough' and her low self-esteem resulting from a specific childhood incident in which she had forgotten to give her pet water and it had died. By resourcing her and connecting her to archetypes of forgiveness through breath, gesture and movement in her body until her bodily gesture became one of peace, confidence and loving self-acceptance, Anna was given tools to follow up on a daily basis in her body, to maintain the gains she had made in the counselling session. This included affirming gestures, sounds and drawings as well as visualizing a healthy pregnancy. I did not see Anna again but I cried when I heard she had delivered a healthy baby and I sensed it was a turning point in her life. She had realized the power of herself to courageously dare to win her life's dreams using her own power and standing on her own ground. She had touched my spirit with the power of herself to recover itself. I was but the midwife honoured to witness the birthing of herself and her own power to shape her life.

Summary of the outcomes of healthy and unhealthy personal growth

1. I am more present in my daily life

In this case study, Anna becomes less present to mobilizing her resources to sustain the pregnancy because she is distracted and emotionally alarmed by the knowledge given to her from the past that portrays her as a perpetrator who is now paying the consequences. Whether or not the knowledge is accurate is less relevant than the lack of awareness on the part of the psychic that such information is unhelpful to the client in her present vulnerable and emotionally fragile position.

The physical and etheric fragility of the client was ignored and there was no recognition that her life forces were preoccupied with building the body of the new child using the resources drawn from her body. To load down the client with more astral or emotional material, which is catabolic and burns up the life forces, was unskilful and this lack of awareness led the client's body to break out into psychosomatic rashes which occur when the astral body carrying the imprints of trauma penetrate the physical body.

Another way of expressing this is to say that the catabolic or breakdown processes of the astral body exceeded the building-up life processes. This makes the client fragile and struggle to be present in the present moment because the trauma system is too close to the surface of the client's day-to-day experience as the energetic boundaries have been corroded.

The client has inadequate preparation to deal with the material that is extracted by the psychic. It would be more skilful for the client to prepare themselves to step over their own inner threshold to their own inner experiences with skilled support, rather than creating a psychic connection which can go badly wrong if the information released by the psychic is indigestible to the under-resourced client, of which Anna's case study is a case in point.

2. I am empowered to shape my destiny

The psychic's information disempowered Anna from dealing with her fears and increased her sense of being a victim of circumstances outside of her control. The self governing 'I' striving towards high levels of self-integration and insight is not supported by the psychic model of personal growth. The psychic, not the client, is the centre of the action and this very structure, regardless of the sensitivity of the psychic, does not predispose this pathway to empower the 'I' in self-sustaining ways. The psychic initiates the change process by determining what information and directions should be given to the client who remains in the passive role, too often exacerbating the client's feelings of weakness, vulnerability and uncertainty. Again this weakens the 'I' which is the single greatest resource the client has to mobilize to change the self-defeating pattern and to transform their fears into the substance of courage.

3. I am increasingly free from reactions

The psychic predications around Anna's threatened miscarriage increased her reactive feelings of anger, fear and abandonment and were not helpful to moving her to a place of self-esteem and self-care. Each time a core decision in one's life is made by somebody else then the will is weakened and the presence of the will is core in this model to a strongly incarnated 'I' in the body. Furthermore, if the client receives unexpected or shocking news, as occurred in this case study, then this can result in the 'I' rapidly leaving the body and exposing the client to the astral and trauma system with all its unintegrated and undigested fears.

4. I am more fully who I am: 'self-actualization' and 'self-transcendence'

Here, the psychic's approach did not support the maturing of the client's 'I' nor increase the client's sense of safety and connectedness with the world. Psychic knowledge was very undermining in this client's case and led her to closing down to the world and fearing her own out of control body.

The holistic model of personal growth for body, soul and spirit: The consequences

Psychics do not connect the client to their highest resources as an integral part of their work because the structure of the psychic session is that the client gives up on their own power to access their deepest sources of insight and power resident in the 'I', and elevates the psychic to this position with in their psyche. This is weakening to healthy psychological growth.

In psychic work , because of the absence of the client's 'I' governing the process, there is always the possibility that the astral information revealed will exceed the client's capacity to digest and assimilate it skilfully into their present life. Psychics run the personal-growth process with their 'I' at the centre and expose the vulnerable client to their assessment of the client's ability to digest information, which may or may not be accurate.

Psychic personal-growth processes are not generally well-integrated into the client's current life, as it is too often focused on future predictions. The purpose of psychic visits is to uncover information for the client, but we need to be very clear that this is achieved with an element of risk and possible emotional flooding with its associated anxiety and stress for the client. Here, we have the psychic penetrating the first threshold of the client's interior life, the threshold that takes the client to the inner knowledge of who they are in all its shades of goodness and darkness.

The psychic pathway tends to overly enlarge the upper pole of thinking without adequate balance or grounding in willing. Often, there is inadequate digestion of the information provided to the client about their problem or predicament. When the feeling life is inadvertently flooded as an unanticipated consequence of the psychic pathway, then the client is left to find a life raft back to safe land, and away from the rising unleashed emotional waters.

Conclusion

The psychic pathway to personal growth, regardless of the psychic's sensitivity to specific clients' emotional vulnerability, is unsupportive of sustainable personal growth because it replaces the clients' 'I' which should be the centre of meaning creation for the client, with the psychic's 'I'. It involves somebody else penetrating the first threshold behind which are hidden all the shadow states, unprocessed and indigestible experiences in the client's unconscious. The threshold to the inner life requires deep preparation and skilful tools to enable the client to enter it skilfully and productively, and such preparation does not occur when a psychic is consulted. This can lead to emotional vulnerabilities, flooding and in serious cases post-traumatic stress disorder as the boundary of the first threshold is breached and the client's defence mechanisms bypassed. Lieviegoed advises on the crossing of the first threshold where the lesser guardian, who is no other than our own unacknowledged, unintegrated experiences, resides:

> The guardian impresses on man that should he wish
> to pass him, man has to be able to assume the task
> hitherto fulfilled by the guardian. He will now have to
> take responsibility himself for his own development,
> free of fear...make every effort to control his drives
> and desires and to apply himself only to positive tasks.
> (Lieviegoed, 1985:p.94)

In breaching this first threshold, the psychic, however accurate, becomes karmically enmeshed in the responsibility for the information uncovered and revealed prematurely to the client. This will have profound consequences not only for the client, but also for the psychic not just in the immediate meeting, but in any future connections.

7. Guides as pathway

We thought because we had power, we had wisdom.
— Stephen Vincent Benet

In western culture, spirit guides, popular in the latter part of the nineteenth century when séances and mediumship flourished, have had a revival in the personal-growth movement of the last thirty years. In conversation today, it is not uncommon to hear a person say that they are undertaking some change in their lives because their 'guide' or 'guides' have told them to do it, which has been delivered to them through their own channelling or mediumship abilities, or by consulting another medium or channeller. A person will speak about their contact with their spirit guide and they will say that they act as channel or medium for the guide to speak through. Other people avidly follow a particular channel or medium that they trust and who delivers personal or cosmic information to them from a guide or spirit. There is a burgeoning book and audio-visual market based around channelled messages from spirit guides from this planet, other planets and galaxies, or from the cosmos. Although channelling presents as a contemporary phenomena, it needs to be remembered that from the Ancient Egyptian temples of Isis to the ancient Greek temples of Delphi, whole communities and cultures relied upon the abilities of select individuals to channel messages from the spiritual world to the human population. Mediumship and channelling were the human lifelines to the world of the gods.

The desire to have contact with the invisible, non-material world remains strong even in contemporary secular and materialistic society. It is estimated that 25–45% or the western population report having had paranormal experiences (Gallup & Newport, 1991, cited in Goudling & Parker, 2001), and 35–50% reported a belief in the existence of paranormal phenomena (West, 1995, cited in Goudling & Parker, 2001). The paranormal includes extra-sensory perception, defined as the perception of people and events not observable as material realities and psychokinesis, or the ability to have an impact on non-material phenomena and the ability to communicate with such realms. A channeller or medium is defined in the Encyclopaedia of Psychic Science as: 'an intermediary for communication between the material and spirit world' (Fodor, 2008). Almost 30% of Americans believe in genuine mediums (Newport & Strausberg, 2001), while 10% of Britons regularly visit them (Roe, 1998). These statistics exist despite the failure of research to validate mediumistic abilities (O'Keefe & Wiseman, 2005). It needs to be acknowledged that it is difficult to research, measure and record non-material experiences with material measuring instruments. It is a little like asking a giant earth-bound turtle to test run and trial the wings of an eagle.

Channellers and mediums claim to leave or make space within their physical body to allow other non-physical beings, spirits or entities to have conversations with human beings about a range of topics, from an individual's love life, personal relationships or workplace, to topics embracing the past, present or future of an individual, a community or the planet. It is believed by mediums that these 'spirit guides' have superior wisdom compared to incarnated human beings and therefore bring knowledge, perspective and insight to solve problems that are beyond the human being's ability to do so with the same effectiveness and insight. These entities or 'spirit guides' are said to read the energy patterns around a person and their life processes so they can give guidance to the person from a broad perspective. Some people will not act until they have contacted their spirit guide for advice on a course of action. For some people, this includes the minute details of their life down to what to eat, wear, who to visit, where to work and live. For other people, the focus is upon the general purpose of their lives and/or the future of the planet.

Channellers and mediums advertise their services to other people and these services can include face-to-face contact, absent readings, or Internet or telephone readings. Increasing numbers of people are seeking access to messages from channellers or mediums, while increasing numbers of people are claiming to be channels or mediums. Some specialize. Doreen Virtue has become famous as a channel for angel guides, and has created many sets of cards representing the positive qualities of the angels she has contacted, which are one of the most popular styles of inspirational card packs on the market today. Barbara Anne Clow claims to specialize in channelling from extra-terrestrial spirit guides, especially from the systems of Pleiades and Sirius. A range of contemporary, personal-growth books on subjects as diverse as physical health to intergalactic contacts and the future of the planet, claim to be channelled by a diverse range of writers.

Fodor (2008) states that mediums have this ability as a result of hereditary or physical /mental health crises in their lives, which have opened them up to the spirit world. In essence, it means that both thresholds, but in particular the second threshold, is easily navigable by these people. They can readily move from the human world to the invisible spiritual world. While this can enable them to access information easily about another person by penetrating the first threshold of the inner life or reach spirits above the second threshold, it means that their relatively transparent thresholds expose them to very large amounts of inside information, a diversity of spiritual energies both good and bad; and a huge spiritual responsibility to discern what is skilful to reveal to others and what is unskilful and damaging to reveal to others. One could describe such abilities as resulting in spiritual pressure and they are seriously error prone if not accompanied by the transformation of their own states of sympathy and antipathy, and the transformation of their own shadow states, which are found in sentient soul which is across their first threshold. Otherwise, their own unprocessed inner material will consciously or unconsciously drive the shaping of the messages they receive and the way they are communicated to the client. Messages from across the threshold are bound to be distorted when the medium's states of sentient soul are like muddy water rather than like a clear, still, forest pool.

Leshan (2003:p.43) explores in depth the processes by which people conduct mediumship and notes that like the mystical experience, mediums gain information in a more sophisticated way than that which is limited to the five human senses. Like the mystic, they become part of the fundamental unity of all things and like the most contemporary quantum physicists note the illusionary nature of current-time models of past, present and future, realizing that everything coexists in the present moment (Leshan 2003:p.87). In addition, Leshan points out that, in the experience of the medium, neither space nor time can prevent energy or information transfer between two individual objects or people. Knowledge comes from tuning into the pattern of things of which one is part. Most significantly, he claims that in the mediumistic experience of reality, there is no free will, only the exploration of pre-existing patterns:

> Free will does not exist since what will be is, [sic]
> and the beginning and end of all enfold each other.
> Decisions cannot be made as these involve action in
> the future and the future is an illusion. One cannot
> take action but can only participate in the pattern of
> things (Leshan, 2003:pp.86f)

This view determines a person's fate and can predispose a person with this view to a disempowered, almost fatalistic, acceptance of their lives. Such a view is not conducive to personal-growth practices, although it may open up the possibilities to seeing contemporary patterns as having preceding causes in other lives.

The promised benefits

People who channel claim to experience a greater feeling of certainty about their lives, which they now feel are guided by expert spiritual advice, rather than by their own mundane human consciousness. Such people feel that following direction from spirit guides enables them to avoid making mistakes in their lives that will result in trauma, and provides the most insightful directions for their behaviour. This pattern of referring to the experts — to take control of one's health, religion, family, relationships and to define how these should be so they will be happy — is a common human behaviour to avoid fear, self-responsibility, uncertainty and the existential angst in decision making. In the field of channelling, the experts are seen as belonging to the spiritual world, which is believed, hierarchically, to be above the human world in consciousness, insight and capacity to direct one's growth and growth. It is assumed that these spiritual beings have higher consciousness and, therefore, know better about what is good for the individual.

The matter is more psychologically complicated when individuals themselves become channels, rather than consult other people as channels. These individuals can experience a type of spiritual pride, in that they have been chosen as the vehicles for these beings of higher consciousness. This sets them apart from ordinary human beings and elevates them to a 'special status'. This is particularly the case for those individuals who choose to create businesses and consultancies based on their channelling abilities. Tuttle, in his famous treatise on Mediumship and its Laws written in the early 1900s, is careful to point out the need for personal training and study of the phenomena in depth, in order to provide the highest level of mediumship. He cautions about the hazards of mediumship for people seeking to make a quick livelihood and or achieve notoriety. Tuttle (n.d., p.34) argues that the quality of the channelling will depend on the character and quality of the medium. Only those mediums that in thought, desire and culture live in the highest light will attract spirits from the highest light. People driven by low motivation, seeking quick incomes, with little culture or deep spiritual aspiration, will channel spirits of a corresponding level of coarseness and self-centredness. True mediumship of the highest order must be a result of prolonged study, inner discipline and the highest and purest spiritual aspirations. It is regrettable that today many people without any training, spiritual or otherwise, are free to deliver their services to unaware clients seeking guidance through the morass of their life's problems. Consequently, it is rather like a game of Russian roulette for the client, as to whether they find a medium who is able to connect them to the spiritual potential of their highest self, or whether they find someone who provides information and energetic connections that are actually depleting and/or damaging for the client. It is essential that clients seeking mediums check out their training, formal and informal, as well as look deeply into the countenance of the medium to see to what degree the light is manifest through their eyes, particularly in relation to the qualities of altruism, purity, compassion and kindness. The accuracy of the client's assessment depends on their ability to 'ego-sense' the moral quality of another person.

The hidden costs

Furthermore, people who are channels or mediums* for guides or spirit are prone to locate themselves in intellectual soul, and bypass the important work needing to be done in their own astrality. One must deal with aversions, desires and reactions all located in sentient soul or the astrality. These are the primary substance of human experiences. These cannot be bypassed in the pursuit of higher orders of experience. When people ignore the astrality in hopes of a quick ascent to the spirit, they are prone to spiritual pride as they begin to see themselves as special or above other people. In the long-term, spiritual pride becomes the foundation for delusion, exploitation or narcissism, all great blocks to healthy personal growth.

In addition, channels may claim to have direct contact with the realms of spirit, to have penetrated the second threshold and to be a conduit for great spiritual beings such as the Archangel Michael, Buddha, Christ, St Germaine, the Ascended Masters, the Great White spirit, Archangel Gabriel, St Joan of Arc, or the Great White Brotherhood. Unfortunately, such exalted status and identity can lead many channels to egoistical behaviour driven by their unprocessed astrality. Attempts to penetrate the second threshold, beyond which these spirit beings are said to reside, by people who have not completed adequate inner growth within their basic human astrality, and transformed emotions of aversion, desire, attachment, will lead to compromising behaviour around greed, sexuality and power. Trying to access the realms of the spirit without being first grounded in one's own self and having cleared one's astrality, is like building a stairway to the spirit in the air, instead of firmly anchoring it upon he ground. If a person has not transformed their own shadow prior to penetrating the second threshold, they are at risk of not being able to discern the shadow spirits from the light spirits. Steiner (1994:p.175) cautions people about prematurely forcing their way through the second threshold because 'forces hostile to life' previously hidden, may become dangerous if they are approached with arrogance and ignorance in the unbridled search to claim power from beyond the second threshold.

Messages from this realm can be relayed through the channel as imperatives for human beings to follow, but if the source is questionable, so must be the message. If the channel has no awareness of the source in relation to the shadow or the light, it is of concern that vulnerable people receive the message without discernment. Tuttle is extremely concerned about poor quality mediumship:

... mediums imperfectly controlled by uncultured
spirits have been productive of the most deplorable
results ... too often the ignorant accept the vague
utterance received from a moving table, or of a trance
medium as infallible authority, and allow the current of
their lives to be changed thereby. They are filled with
the vain conceit that they are specially ordained for
missions ... unless the spirit realm can be approached
with unbiased judgment and uncompromising reason
it becomes dangerous ground ... irresponsible spirit
intelligence that impels its blind devotees, not in the
course of right, but in the opposite direction. (Tuttle,
n.d., p.38)

He goes on to argue that mediums attract spirits to
them that reflect their level of spiritual work, particularly
their conquest of their astral or animal desires, cravings
and aversions. Possession of the medium by negative, dark,
controlling, egotistical spirits is only a risk for mediums that
have such conditions already within themselves:

As eagles seek the mountain heights, leaving darksome
caverns for noisome reptiles, bats, owls, spirit
intelligences who are good seek those who reach
upward to the heights, and those who have not
outgrown their animal propensities attract intelligences
of a lower order (Tuttle, p.39)

There is also the age-old problem of fraudulent practice,
which is not restricted to mediums and channels. However,
because of the difficulty in validating the information that a
channel or medium communicates, even inter-subjectively,
— that is, two people attempting to channel the same

information and cross-checking whether their experience is similar — clients can be seriously misled and inaccurate information provided. In the parapsychology research field Palmer (cited in Wiseman et al, 1995:p.15) states that 'Psychic fraud has been the single most important factor in damaging the reputation of parapsychology and retarding its growth.' Wiseman (1995:p.16) points to mediumistic frauds initially undetected in the research of Project Alpha in the United States, and the resultant defunding and negative publicity attached to such fraudulent practices. Wiseman (1995:pp.53f) goes on to list types of trickery and cheating uncovered in the process of research on mediums, which are cause for caution among users of psychics as a personal-growth pathway, as much as for researchers trying to explicate the psychic experience. These include checking out other ways in which the medium may have found the information that they are presenting, and being aware of potential signs of trickery by which they elicit information by indirect means. A typical example is a comment like: 'Someone you know has died (we all know someone who has died). Tell me have you lost a relative or friend or acquaintance?'

Characteristics of healthy personal growth

1. Promotes the growth of autonomous 'I'
Channelling does not promote the growth of an autonomous 'I' rather the reverse, the 'I' of the channeller or the person who relies on a channeller to make their life decisions abnegates their self-responsibility and autonomy to the spirit guide. One of the primary costs of either becoming a channel or consulting a channel about one's life decisions, is increasing dependence on a source of

information external to the person. This is the basis for disempowerment of the individual's self and weakens the individual's self-ownership and self-decision-making around their lives. The consequence of this is a loss of integration of the self or 'I', weakening the individual's growth and undermining confidence in their own insight. This results in an abnegation of one's own growth and decision-making and giving it over to some external force, in this case a spirit guide. This can create chronic dependency and co-dependency where the person lacks confidence to make decisions without advice from the spiritual guides. Such co-dependency is very difficult to break and identify. Such co-dependency with a human partner, with an institution, can be more readily identified and worked with. Some supernatural status is associated with spirit guides, beyond the human world, which makes it very difficult to identify and develop the confidence to challenge and reclaim responsibility for one's own deeds.

Channellers speak about leaving their bodies, or moving aside for the spirit guide. The Encyclopaedia of Psychic Sciences, which has contributions from a range of well known mediums, notes some of the experiential costs to the channeller's autonomy and well-being of this process. Physical exhaustion and depletion following possession by the spirit guide is experienced in the physical and emotional body and may also be experienced by the audiences who consult channellers, who use the client's energy to sustain the channelling process (Fodor, 2008). Essentially, this means that the channelling process can cost life force or vitality, so it is potentially unsuitable for people already suffering from low vitality.

2. Emphasizes the client's capacity as initiator of processes
Stainton Moses notes the hazards in mediumship of the client getting into relationship with a positive spiritual guide:

> In developing mediumship one has to consider a question involving three serious points. Can you get into relation with a spirit who is wise enough and strong enough to protect and good enough for you to trust? If you do not you are exposed to that recurrent danger which the old occultists used to describe as the struggle with the dweller on the threshold. It is true that everybody who crosses the threshold of this occult knowledge does unquestionably come into a new and strange land in which, if he has no guide, he is apt to lose his way. (Fodor, 2008. www.spiritwritings.com/ fodor.html)

Mediumship involves crossing the second threshold. This threshold, takes us from the human world to the spiritual world and is particularly hazardous if the first threshold, the world of each individual's interior experiences with all there shades of darkness and light both from this life and other lives, has not yet been adequately transformed. As Steiner emphasizes, the critically important task is to transform the guardian of the first threshold, the guardian that is a representation of all of our deeds, black, white and grey, and which he describes as speaking to each one of us personally: 'I am your own creation ... You have formed me but by so doing you have undertaken to transform me' (Lievegoed, 1985:p.94). If the intending medium has not undertaken adequate inner work to transform their own shadow states then, in crossing the second threshold, they can easily lose control over the channelling process, and can be overtaken involuntarily by 'spirit guides' of a similar nature to their unprocessed shadow material. It then flows down to clients who consult them, who may find that the messages they are given are contaminated, misguided and misdirected by spirits of a shadow order. Unless the client is very skilful in critiquing the quality of these messages, they may be easily duped. The greatest immunity from such a duping is for the client to work diligently to transform their own shadow states, their own aversions and desires in their astral bodies. Then they can critique from an 'I' position rather than from a position of astral neediness.

3. Provides processes so client can sustain improvements

Channelling and mediumships do not generally provide processes for the client, but rather information or guidance on what the client should or should not do in their daily life, or advice about particular issues in the client's life. Once the mediumship has ceased the client is left to follow through on their own, which can be difficult when dependency on the spirit guide is chronic. Also, there are many cases where the spirit guides are not satisfied in communicating to the client how they should run their life, but insist that they give messages to others to change their lives or behave in certain ways. This is not a client-initiated process, although the client may have exposed themselves initially to the channelling processes and made efforts to contact a spirit guide.

4. Monitors the client to ensure their 'I' can digest and integrate the experiences

Today, monitoring of the medium's ability to digest the process is not regularly part of the process as it was in the past. Fodor (2008) notes that many famous mediums including Marquis Centurione Scotto and Mrs Piper had their mediumship suspended for a number of years by the spirit guide because of their health problems. As previously mentioned, the thinning of the second threshold that mediums cross to commune with the spiritual world, can lead to exhaustion. Also, without having adequately processed their own inner psychological shadow states, it is easy for mediums to lose control of the boundaries between themselves and the 'spirit guide' They then proclaim themselves to be the Archangel Michael, God, Jesus Christ, St Germain or a host of other powerful, spiritual figures and proceed to act according to their new-found, elevated, spiritual identity. In current psychiatric terms, this is identified as psychosis and the person usually ends up in a mental health hospital, because one of the characteristics of this absorption in an elevated spiritual identity is the failure to complete day-to-day human tasks of eating, sleeping and maintaining one's physical lifestyle. During the psychosis, the medium will usually exhibit manic qualities and often have extraordinary amounts of energy for a prolonged period of time and undertake frenetic activity, advising friends, colleagues and relatives what specific course of action they must pursue in their lives to be safe and happy. Eventually, the medium will collapse from exhaustion and a prolonged period of recovery is usually required during which the difficult journey of trying to rebuild the self, and deal with the shadow material in the astrality will need to be undertaken to restore healthy psychological functioning.

The client of the medium in such a state of mental breakdown is vulnerable to misleading information of a high order and being given life directions for change from a voice that speaks with unassailable authority. Even when the client can identify that their medium is out of control, it can be very distressing for vulnerable clients who have projected their unmet needs, particularly for safety and security, onto the medium or channel.

Case study

Julia was an intelligent, sensitive and compassionate fifty-five-year-old woman whose life had encompassed working as an accountant, being mother to four children, being a graphic artist and a businesswoman. She was multi-talented, thoughtful and deeply reflective. Julia was into complementary healing and what she described as a healthy lifestyle. She had always been a deeply spiritual person and although she never attended church she always spoke reverently about not undertaking any major decision without the guidance of spirit and was very committed to following spirit along her personal-growth pathway. She had several close friends and was appreciated by a wide circle of people in her community because of her empathy, kindness and supportive presence. Julia explained to me that before she made any major decision she would always consult with her spirit guide, to ensure that they were made from the highest place.

I had seen Julia in therapy for a routine life issue about five years prior to a very desperate phone call. Julia asked to see me urgently because she was conscious that an 'entity' was trying to take over her and she felt that she was losing control of herself and her life. She said she first experienced the presence of the 'entity' following an intensive spiritual training programme she had undertaken to awaken her third eye. She said the entity would occupy her body and speak through her giving her advice on how to manage her life and the lives of significant other people. However, she had ceased sleeping or eating regularly for over four weeks because of the pervading presence of 'this entity in her body'. She felt unable to resist it even when she decided to stop contact with it. She believed that the entity, called Zepheron, was guiding her life and she began making random phone calls to friends giving them messages from this being.

Julie did not attend the appointment because that day she ended up being admitted to a mental health hospital after the neighbours called the police when she started screaming uncontrollably in the street outside her home, and seemed unable to calm down or respond to reason. She kept telling them that the dark forces were after her. She was admitted to a mental health hospital and diagnosed with psychosis and drugged accordingly in order to quieten her.

Once Julia left hospital she began counselling seeking to ensure that this experience did not happen again. I explained that counselling would be ineffective and useless until we could re-locate the client's 'I' back in her body. I offered suggestions like footbaths with slices of lemon, regular meals and sleeping, lots of walking, and referred her for immediate treatment with a homeopath who had excellent remedies for grounding the client's I' quickly back in their bodies. It required about twelve weeks of recuperation to restore her physical, mental and emotional strength again. During that time, Julia attended counselling sessions and discovered inner patterns of spiritual pride and hatred that made her vulnerable to seeking spiritual expression through mediumship. She made a strong commitment to develop her own place of insight and to become autonomous in directing her own spiritual growth so that such an experience would not recur.

Summary of the outcomes of healthy and

unhealthy personal growth

1. I am more present in my daily life

In channelling, it is clear that when the boundaries dissolve across the second threshold, the channeller becomes less present to their material daily life in all respects as can be seen from the case study above where the Julia even failed to eat and sleep and maintain her day-to-day life needs. In fact, it was as though an alien consciousness with another worldly, non-human agenda was running her life. While the experience is not as intense for consumers of channelled messages, they are still psychologically more and more detached from the present moment as they seek advice from 'guides' who are not human beings. Directions come from some other dimension of consciousness and are not always related skilfully to problems in the day-to-day material world.

In both historical and contemporary channelling, medium fatigue and exhaustion has proved problematic. The more the etheric becomes depleted, the greater the likelihood that the first threshold into the medium's unprocessed inner life will thin and, when this occurs, it can result in flooding of the medium with overwhelming amounts of astral experiences of their own that they have not previously processed. Fodor (2008) notes that, traditionally, many mediums suffered from cravings for stimulants like alcohol in an attempt to overcome the exhaustion following their channelling. The balance between the building-up and breaking-down processes in the human physical body can be difficult to maintain in the channelling experience. Fodor (2008) also indicates that mediums often draw on the energy of the people who have come for a reading, who they refer to as 'sitters'.

> Some mediums draw more of the sitters' vitality than others. These mediums become less exhausted and consequently can sit more often. Mrs Etta Wriedt always left her sitters weak.
> (http://spiritwritings.com/fodor.html)

2. I am empowered to shape my destiny

Mediumship and channelling is antithetical to the development of the autonomous 'I' because it deliberately sets out to bypass , replace or override the channel's 'I', or the client's I', with the 'spirit guide'. In this age of consiousness soul, we are called to take individual responsibility for our own lives and our spiritual transformation. This does not mean we cannot seek assistance, advice or guidance but discretion is essential. In particular, unhealthy processes occur when we give up on directing our own core life choices rather than become motivated and inspired to renew our intentions to transform our lives into healthier and more psychologically whole places.

When clients of channellers and mediums become dependent on channelled messages from 'spirit guides' they become increasingly disempowered to direct their own lives as they hand over direction of their lives to a spirit guide, who they elevate to a higher status of power than themselves. This weakens their 'I' and makes them vulnerable to being manipulated or exploited by such unskilful and unethical 'guides'.

3. I am increasingly free from reactions

In Julia's case of 'spirit guide possession', quite the contrary appeared to happen. As the spirit of the being increasingly possessed her consciousness she was driven by mania, self-righteousness, judgements and other reactive states of mind and there was no space for insight and compassion in her behaviour. This oscillation between reflective insightful 'I'-writing and chaotic commentary from guides is illustrated by comparing and contrasting two books written by Barbara Hand Clow: The Pleiadian Agenda, which is channelled, and The Mayan Code, which is Barbara Hand Clow's compilation of information she has acquired from a number of sources. The Pleiadian Agenda is chaotic and disorganized with one spirit guide after another floating randomly through the book's writing, each spirit guide with its own version of events, often contradicting preceding information offered in the book. The author's organising consciousness is mostly absent; the reader feels like they have been launched on some chaotic route through the galaxy without any space pilot or authorial 'I'. The reader is left to find some meaning from these inchoate convolutions. At times, the advice offered by the 'spirit guide' claiming authorship is questionable, as when it keeps repeating that that there is no such thing as evil on planet Earth only boredom, and any deed is fine provided it relieves the boredom. In contrast, The Mayan Code has a strong presence of the integrated 'I' of Barbara. It is well organized in structure and the content has thematic connections which create whirls and webs of meaning through which the reader can navigate with ease. There is an awareness of other people following similar threads of knowledge and discovery, and the book has a richness of pattern and meaning, regardless of whether one is in agreement or not with its conclusions. As a result of reading it, one is more connected to other humans, planets and galaxies, whereas the result of reading The Pleiadian Agenda is to be trapped in a web of chaotic threads that fail to form a tapestry that could provide clear connectedness to new dimensions of knowledge, experience or human relationships. The two books provide an excellent contrast between a conscious human authorial 'I' writing a book, and an absent 'I' and some random assortment of spirit guides channelling a book. In The Pleiadean Agenda, the author does not seem to notice when the spirit guide's tone of voice change, even when they parade under the same name. In contrast, in The Mayan Code, we are left with the fruits of her presence, her insight into a new dimension of experience that is richly woven into an tapestry that calls our own 'I' and demands an expanded level of human consciousness and connectedness within and around us.

4. I am more fully who I am: 'self-actualization' and 'self-transcendence'

Sanctimoniousness, or spiritual pride, with its associated arrogance separated Julia from others, her family and friends, who were all spoken to as inferiors whose lives need to be directed by her under the mediumship of Zehperon. During the dominance by the 'spirit guide', Julia lost her personal identity and became more and more isolated in her relationships as friends and acquaintances found it impossible to communicate with her in any meaningful way. She was living as though on the other side of the second threshold and indistinguishable in her own mind from Zepheron, who she was convinced was the spirit guiding her channelling. The problem was that Julia was not at the centre of her consciousness or her body. As Ekhart Tolle (Bedson, 2005) noted: 'If the master is not present in the house, all kinds of shady characters will take up residence there.'

The worst result of a negative dominating spirit guide is that they are difficult to rid oneself of, and they can create serious dysfunction in the medium's daily life and family. It was an agonising process for Julia to finally rid herself of the unwanted spirit possession, even when she was clear that she wanted to be free from it. Fodor (2008) notes that some 'entities' will actually take hold of a medium, even when they are unwilling or do not wish to be a medium. Such was the experience of Julia in the case study, as the 'entity' took control of her life against her will.

The holistic model of personal growth for body, soul and spirit: The consequences

Mediumship and the channelling of spirit guides in previous eras and cultures has previously been a process recognised as requiring much training, discipline and community support. People became initiates in order to qualify to be skilful channels of the spiritual world. Unfortunately, in contemporary channelling, such processes, with a few exceptions, are no longer in place to safeguard the medium who is crossing the second threshold to commune with the higher spiritual powers. Too often the medium is not adequately informed or trained and is buffeted by the 'spirit guide or guides' in whatever way the spirit guide chooses. The 'I' in mediumship and channelling is usually displaced by the spirit guide who offers resources from the transpersonal. Some of these resources may support human physical and emotional health and well-being, but some of these resources may undermine it. Only in the degree to which the channel has cleared their own astral material of aversion and desire will they be able to discern the difference.

In mediumship, either as medium or client, it is difficult to cultivate one's own thinking, feeling and willing. One is, therefore, likely as a medium to begin to manifest the qualities of the spirit guide which, if positive, may be desirable, but which, if undesirable, may be ethically costly. Sometimes, mediums' personalities appear to change over time from generous to greedy and so forth, as a result of prolonged exposure to an unhealthy spirit guide. The mature growth of discerning and illumined thinking, warmed by a heart that experiences profound interbeing manifest in ethical actions of compassion, is a delicate personal-growth balance, unlikely to be cultivated through mediumship or channelling.

Conclusion

Channelling, or mediumship, is a complex pathway to personal growth. How one understands it depends on where one locates oneself theoretically. In the clinical model, it is explained it in terms of some type of psychopathology with various types of psychosis, while the cognitive approach sees it as cognitive bias. The neurobiological approach explains it in terms of brain function and dysfunctions while the psi approach states that some people objectively experience what they claim to be experiencing. (Goodling & Parker, 2001:p.75). People who channel or consult mediums tend to believe the channel is actually in contact with the spiritual world of spirit 'guides', who are able to shed greater wisdom on their lives because these guides have higher knowledge than incarnate human beings.

The real challenge is that this pathway is difficult if the spirit guide turns out to be controlling in a destructive ways and it can be very difficult for the susceptible client to get free. Macbeth lives as a reminder of the disasters that can happen to an individual, a family and an empire because one egoistic individual chose to listen to the channelled prediction from the three witches that he should inherit a kingdom. A message in itself is not destructive, but when mixed with the untransformed astral energies of human beings driven by fear, greed, hatred, ignorance, jealousy and other shadow states, it can become a potent and toxic brew both personally and socially.

8. Neo-shamanism as pathway

... All is a circle within me.
I have gone into the earth and out again
I have gone to the edge of the sky.
Now all is at peace within me,
Now all has a place to come home
— Nancy Wood

Neo-shamanism is also known as modern western shamanism or modern European shamanism. It represents a movement in the New Age, beginning in the 1960s, to recapture the interconnectedness of the human being with the natural environment by reconnecting and reviving traditional shamanistic practices that were based on a view of nature as the source of life and immanent with spirit. (Benavides, 1998). Neo-shamanism provides a personal-growth process that restores the mystical experience to the follower, a primal unity with all creation that goes beyond the modern secular world which Weber described as 'a world robbed of Gods' (Von Stuckard, 2002:p.772).

The New Age movement saw the shaman as representing the ability of humans to access spiritual levels of reality and experience, as well as promoting a respectful life toward the sacred web of creation. It is seen as a holistic, inner pathway, available to revitalize estranged urban human beings in western cultures and societies. Traditional shamanism refers to a diverse range of beliefs and practices among indigenous cultures spread across the planet, where the shaman acts as an intermediary between the natural and spiritual world for their community. Shamanism assumes that the visible material world is pervaded by invisible forces or spirits that profoundly affect the lives of the living and must be dialogued with to ensure the well-being of human beings. Walsh defines shamanism as:

> A family of traditions whose practitioners focus on voluntarily entering altered states of consciousness in which they experience themselves or their spirit travelling to other realms at will and interacting with other entities in order to serve their community. (Walsh, 1990:p.11)

Essentially, in traditional shamanism, the shaman can control and cooperate with spirits for the community's benefits. The shaman can treat illnesses or sickness; their soul can leave their body and travel on a shamanic journey to complete certain tasks. They may engage in singing, dancing and music, particularly drumming, sometimes taking psychotropic drugs to enter trance states (Walsh, 2001:p.34). It is interesting to note that indigenous shamanism has gone through a process with western cultures over the past 300 years in which it has been initially demonized, then pathologized, and, finally, through the personal-growth industry, idealized (Hamayon, 1998).

Neo-shamanism provides some very diverse pathways to personal growth depending on which traditional culture or cultures are at its foundation, but all the pathways demonstrate a moulding of traditional shamanic practices

with western anthropological knowledge, and the integration
of neo-pagan elements of ritual particularly in Europe. In
neo-shamanism there is a diminished importance of the
role of community and an increased emphasis on personal
growth and spiritual empowerment among individual
practitioners (Von Stuckard, 2002:p.775). There are also
revitalizing rituals under names as diverse as Sun Dances,
Moon festivals, fire walks, vision quests, that reconnect
the individual transpersonally to the natural world and
its rhythms and energies. In addition, there is a focus on
particular rituals for therapeutic work such as retrieving
soul parts that have been lost through trauma, sucking out
bodily or mental illnesses from the client, finding animals
(totems) or nature guides to answer questions for the client
about a problem, and the like.

The promised benefits

Neo-shamanism provides for a range of benefits to the
practitioners, which include opportunities for a transpersonal
connection with the natural world and the cosmos that
do not require any allegiance or belief in a god or one
controlling deity. Realignment with the rhythms and patterns
of nature promises revitalization to the human soul cut off
from its roots and encaptured in sterile urban environments.
As Halifax notes:

> The sacred languages used during ceremony or
> evoked in various states of consciousness outside
> culture can move teller, singer, and listener out of
> habitual patterns of perception. Indeed speaking
> in the tongues of sea and stone, bird and beast,

or moving beyond language itself is a form of
perceptual healing
(Halifax, 1979:p.92)

The experiential natural world-view is one that rebinds
us to nature, to awaken again the parts of ourselves
that have died in our western segmented, fragmented,
exploitative approach to the relationship between nature
and humans. These themes of reunion with nature are
crystallized in modern western shamanism. We can literally
and metaphorically again walk on fire because shamans
teach one how to recapture the elements within ourselves
that bind us to the earth and to a newly experienced
cosmic unity. Shamans go beyond the limitations of
material appearances, to the energetic patterns that dance
and weave behind them.

Therapists have become interested in incorporating
shamanic journeys into therapy techniques in western
psychotherapy and there have been preliminary studies
indicating the benefits on well-being and immune responses
of the shamanic journey (Harner & Tyron, 1996). Finally,
the personal-growth pathway offered by shamans can
show western people how to experience a deep profound
unity with nature, and with the universe that can best be
described as mystical, and which leaves the participant
knowing experiences of transcendence. Harner (1985)
claims that 90% of people are able to undertake shamanic
journeys without difficulty, so it provides a pathway to
relatively easily accessed altered states of consciousness
and experience.

The hidden costs

Kehoe (2000) is highly critical of the western appropriation of shamanism. The problem with taking something from another culture is that it is often a random and incomplete process of selection. Traditional shamanism is a very complex practice involving many years of training and initiation in indigenous culture to qualify for this position. Diluted by western practitioners and grafted onto a medley of other elements the result is a potpourri of which some elements are known and some are unknown. This neo-shamanistic practice may result not only in disrespecting the traditional shamanism but also in practices that are downright dangerous or risky to people who are inadequately prepared or initiated. So, for example, certain rituals may invoke certain spirits at inappropriate times and raise their anger. Shamanism in its traditional sense, can provide practitioners with the power to penetrate both the first threshold of the interior knowledge of another human being, and also the second threshold of the realms of cosmic consciousness. It is a journey with powerful destinations and the traditional shaman undergoes profound initiation experiences to prepare them for what they may encounter along the way.

Western people, incompletely trained, unaware of the hazards of crossing these thresholds within human consciousness, may experiment blithely with shamanism in ways and situations that traditional practitioners would view with caution or taboo. Western people seem unaware that the greatest dangers to our mental health and well-being are not visible, but invisible and inappropriate, or that ignorant use of these forces may have damaging effects on a person's well-being. Hence, individuals following piecemeal shamanic practices may err with danger to themselves and others because of incomplete knowledge of the forces with which they are experimenting. In addition, certain elements of the tradition may be overlooked or deleted by western practitioners of Shamanism to the detriment of recipients of shamanic practices. An example is the complete lack of awareness of the negative consequences of the spirits that a particular ritual is invoking. Harmer (1980:p.136) notes the denial of negative spirits or the pretence of ignoring of them by many western practitioners. Also, the tendency in western shamanism is to believe that everybody can practise shamanistic rituals, often overlooking the necessary psychic and cultural preparation. In indigenous cultures, shamanistic practices are restricted to the few who have undergone the appropriate training or initiation and who have manifested the particular vocational signs for shamanism in their experiences. Half-skilled professionals are always potentially dangerous because they don't know what they don't know.

Characteristics of Healthy Personal growth

1. Promotes the growth of autonomous 'I'

Shamanism as a pathway does not emphasize the growth of the individual autonomous 'I' or place of insight, as much as the practices which connect a person to other non-human types of powerful consciousnesses, whether animal, spirit or otherwise, to augment their human knowledge and power and provide them with additional knowledge and power, not otherwise accessible by the human being in a normal state of mind. The focus is not upon developing an autonomous 'I' but on fusing into, and with, other forms of supra-human consciousness. In its best form, this may give a person a transpersonal experience that enlarges their own conscious awareness and, in its least functional aspects, it can produce states of mind that would be labelled, in western medicine, as psychotic, and which prevent the individual from functioning sufficiently to care for their day-to-day needs as a human being.

2. Emphasizes the client's capacity as initiator of processes

In Shamanistic processes, the client gives themselves over to the expert shaman after identifying their problem and requesting assistance. In group shamanic processes or rituals, the client does not initiate the process, and they are dependent on the facilitator's skills to safely and skilfully enter altered states of consciousness and return as a functioning human being.

3. Provides processes so client can sustain improvements

Shamanic processes are extremely diversified and some provide tools to teach the client to effect and sustain a change, and other processes simply leave the client without any way of managing the change process and this can result in extraordinary stress to the client.

4. Monitors the client to ensure their 'I' can digest and integrate the experiences

This is highly variable and dependent upon the skills and training of the particular practitioner or group facilitator. Generally, a follow-up after group experiences is low in western personal-growth culture so many of the effects of a particular shamanic journey, both positive and negative, do not emerge until some days or weeks after the process. This lack of continuity in western shamanism raises important concerns for the safety of people undergoing some of the processes offered by some western shamanistic practitioners, particularly in the medium and long-term when the clients are on their own, living with the consequences of a particular initiation or experience.

Case study

I will now illustrate through a composite case study what can go wrong with the shamanistic approach to a problem, in this case stopping smoking,

Justine was from Germany and fifty years old when she decided she just had to give up smoking. She had four grown children, lived alone and had no history of adverse mental health. Justine had already followed the quick-fix trail. She had tried patches, hypnotherapy and prescribed drugs to stop smoking and nothing had worked for more than a few weeks. She was getting desperate because she had begun to feel its adverse effects on her physical health: shortness of breath, scratchy throat and a nasty hacking cough in the mornings.

She was motivated to change and answered an ad in the newspaper by someone offering a cure for smoking. All that was required was one hour and $190 with a money-back guarantee that you would stop smoking. The advertisement promised that this method would definitely work. Justine booked an appointment and arrived at the practitioner's room to be greeted by a middle-aged, bearded man who claimed to work as a shamanistic healer (no mention of this in the advertisement). During the hour she was with him, he asked for very detailed information about her life, which included all her biographical details, her date of birth, her astrological details and all the key events that had happened to her. Detailed notes were taken for over forty minutes about her life biography and he appeared to be working out mathematical numbers from details she gave him.

Upon completion of the interview, he repeated a number of prayers accompanied by the use of bellows which he said was his conduit to the universe and God, who would remove the evil spirit that was causing the smoking. For a week after the treatment, Justine felt free of the urge to smoke. She had extra energy and began jogging daily and felt a new person now that the smoking craving had disappeared. She was delighted with the results and believed that soon her health would recover form her life-long smoking addiction, which had commenced at the age of thirteen years.

However, at the end of the first week, she started to have bad dreams and her sleep became very troubled. Her voice started to change and become flat and monotonous and she stopped feeling like herself, describing that she felt emotionless and without any spiritual protection. At about the same time, she dreamt she heard a voice saying 'we've got you now' and she awoke feeling very uneasy and seriously lacking in any energy or motivation. She then experienced mental confusion, unable to focus on the present moment, unsteady in her walking, unable to make any decisions because of a grey mental haze around and within her head. She was so disoriented and dysfunctional that she could not conduct her daily life activities. In fear and terror she retreated into her home and did not speak to anyone for several days. Friends became very concerned about her because she had become incoherent in her speech and dysfunctional in her day-to-day behaviour. As Christian fundamentalists, they encouraged her to seek the help of a Christian minister to pray over her and remove any of the evil influences that had afflicted her. Justine claims that after having been prayed over her life became more functional and she could undertake her daily tasks more easily. However, she still experienced difficulty in thinking and, in particular, any task involving organization, logic or planning. She felt her creativity had disappeared and her energy and motivational levels were extremely low as if 'part of her spirit had been sucked out of her body'.

It was three months after her encounter with the shamanistic smoking healer, that she presented in counselling. She had resumed smoking about one month after the promised cure. The healer had offered her the opportunity to recontact him if she ever had the craving to smoke again but she was too fearful of the healer and his methods to contact him again. She came to counselling not to give up smoking but to recover from her experience with the quick-fix smoking healer and, in particular, to reclaim back the parts of herself that she experienced as having gone missing. She felt that she was under some dire curse that was immobilizing her life.

She completed three counselling therapy sessions using the somatically based psychotherapy outlined in holistic counselling (Sherwood, 2007). This is a counselling process based on the anthroposophically model that actively engages the 'I' or integrated self in every step of the process. Her intention for the first session in therapy was to remove her guilt. The first session was to strengthen her 'I', her sense of self-worth, by transforming the guilt about allowing herself to undertake the healing to compassionate understanding and self-acceptance. The second session worked around his intention ('statement of her 'I') not to feel fearful of the healer any more. This involved teaching her how to keep her to remain in her body by not allowing her 'I ' to leave through fear. It was critical to stop the dissociation because in those times she had little memory of material events happening around her and felt extremely ungrounded, powerless and vulnerable. Fear can only occur when the 'I' dissociates. When the 'I' or integrated self, which is also the place of insight, remains in the body, then the client has the power to integrate the experience into the self in a functional way. In this session. the invasions she experienced in her body by the healer were removed as her primary wish had been to overcome her fear of the healer.

In the last session, her wish was to recover the parts of her mind and her body that she experienced energetically as missing. Through an active process involving gesture, sound, visualization and movement these were reclaimed by the client so that she felt whole and complete again. After the third session, she stated that she had almost returned to normal functioning prior to her adverse experience with the healer. Two years later, Justine reported to have maintained the parts of herself she had reclaimed in the session and to be functioning well. However, she was still smoking. She may have benefited from meditation practices to reduce her stress responses underlying her smoking or by body-based processes including such complementary health practices as acupuncture or acupressure to relieve the craving for nicotine. Whatever the solution was for her smoking problem, it was going to take some time.

Summary of the outcomes of healthy and unhealthy personal growth

We will now evaluate the outcomes of this shamanistic smoking cessation process in terms of the established outcomes for healthy psychological growth.

1. I am more present in my daily life

This shamanistic personal-growth options did not support more presence of the client in her day-to-day life. The client underwent processes with little awareness or insight into what was happening. There was more presence immediately after the shamanistic process but this was short-lived. So, for example ,Justine was free for one week from her smoking habit and experienced being very present in her body with high levels of well-being. However, this gain was temporary and, after one week, Justine found that she was so dissociated from the reality of day-to-day life that she could not function in her daily life to meet her day-to-day living tasks. This was a very big regression from her previous level of day-to-day functioning in her life. She was not more present in her life in any way after the first week, on the contrary; she was now focused on the past, and on how much she had lost of herself.

2. I am empowered to shape my destiny

After the initial week, Justine experienced great fear and terror over the loss of control over her life both in terms of managing and organizing her life and in feeling flooded and helpless. The intensity of disempowerment was so substantial that she was forced to seek further help to recover her previous level of functionality. Justine was not empowered by this process to take control over her life in any way. If the craving to smoke recurred, the healer could only advise her to return to him over and over again until the craving stopped. She had no self-management tools and felt profoundly disempowered by the whole experience. At the centre of processes was not the autonomous 'I' or integrated self of the client, but rather the 'I' of the healer and any other attached spirits that he had invoked, which in Justine's case were not helpful spirits. Personal growth in which the 'I' of the client is not the self-managing centre will weaken rather than strengthen the position of the 'I' or insightful self. As a consequence, this weakens the whole life of the client, because the 'I' is the highest part of the human being and it set the vibrational patterns for the astral, etheric and physical. If the 'I' is flooded there is a tendency to dissociate (as in the case study of Justine) leaving the client unable to manage their life effectively.

In the case study, Justine did express the conscious intention to give up smoking but the shaman did not empower her to work towards self-managing her wish. Rather, he created a process which increased her dependence on him and that radically reduced her will, her basic day-to-day functioning self, and appeared to eliminate parts of her mind including her organizational skills, her focusing, her mental energy and her self-confidence. This resulted in a reduced sense of self, weakened will and lowered self-motivation for the client and adversely affected her personal growth.

If the shaman is to govern the process rather than the client's 'I' then the shaman needs to have some control over his own 'I' and the type of spirits he is invoking, and of the potentially destructive, as well as constructive, spirits that he accesses.

3. I am increasingly free from reactions

As a result of losing much of her day-to-day functional capacity, Justine become very fearful that she had done the wrong thing in seeing the healer, and her childhood fundamentalist background came to the fore again. In addition to her smoking problem, Justine had now compounded problems associated with her fear of losing her mind and her guilt at having become involved with the healer. The level of her reactive states of mind and feeling had actually increased following the treatment. She experienced less equanimity and peace in her life and a higher level of unproductive, destabilizing reactive states.

Due to Justine's flooding with fear and terror, she dissociated so quickly after the first week that she recounts large periods of memory loss and emotional numbness when she could not even feel her body She describes this state as though her spirit had been sucked away from her. This exacerbated her panic and fear and left her feeling vulnerable and unsafe. It was during this period that she dreamt of voices threatening to take her over. Finally, there was no understanding of the need to balance Justine's will to stop smoking with her fragile emotional state and unhappy thought processes. There was no integration into the feeling level of Justine's experience, that is, why did she smoke? On the thinking level: How did her thought processes maintain the habit? Such a process had limited capacity to work towards an integrated personal-growth process with Justine to support her to give up smoking.

4. I am more fully who I am: 'self-actualization' and 'self-transcendence'

Justine clearly experienced having less of her integrated self following the shamanic personal-growth process for smoking, than prior to undertaking it. In fact, she felt so little of herself was left that she consciously sought healing and counselling to recover herself. Within one month of the smoking treatment, she not only had returned to smoking but felt fragmented in herself, and unable to integrate the experience and insisted that pieces of herself had been removed and were missing, and that she could not longer complete tasks that she had been competent to do prior to meeting the shaman.

In terms of approaching transcendence and feeling more connected to herself, others and the world, Justine experienced the reverse, needing to retreat into herself, feeling unable to connect with others in her day-to-day world. In essence, this shamanistic intervention offered remarkable changes but these were not sustainable in the long-term and in the case of Justine, actually resulted in a lower level of self-integration and self-functioning in the world in the medium and long-term than prior to the shamanistic intervention.

The holistic model of personal growth for body, soul and spirit: The consequences

In shamanistic processes, the client is dependent on the expertise of the facilitator to navigate a safe way in and out of altered states of consciousness and other non-human consciousnesses. If the shaman is incompetent, the consequences for the client can be dire, including feeling that one has become possessed by other forms of consciousness, or one has lost part of one's consciousness. These consequences may not be easily reversible. However, if the practitioner is skilled then particularly difficult illnesses may be reversed, including mental health disorders and effective shamanistic interventions aim to restore harmony between humans and nature which may require communication with spirits that are causing discord and disease (Turner, 1982:p.132).

In some traditional shamanism, there was clear awareness that only robust individuals with a strong anabolic constitution would be suitable to undertake and maintain shamanic training. There was also the awareness in many traditions that an illness was often necessary to provide initiation into shamanic practices. However, in contemporary western shamanism there is a view that almost anyone can undertake shamanic experiences of some type and there is little real assessment of the person's physical and emotional state of health, or the potential consequences of the client's exposure to a radical new state of consciousness that crosses the second threshold in the medium and long-term.

Furthermore, in western culture there are no support communities in place for individuals who become flooded after being exposed to materials from shamanic processes. Follow-up after shamanistic workshops or individual sessions is not well organized and most individuals would be left unsupported with material that arises. Leaving a person in this distressed state is too common in shamanistic processes in the west, and the lack of professional associations with rigorous training criteria to enforce practice standards is of real concern to people considering shamanistic personal-growth options. In western society, uncontrollable altered states of consciousness will generally result in being admitted to psychiatric wards and treated as a psychiatric patient.

It is clear in the holistic counselling model that shamanistic practices are attempting to transcend the second threshold, that is, the threshold that connects humans with the invisible realms. Without adequate inner preparation for dealing with the psychological issues that are stored within the individual in the astrality, this exposes both the healer and the client to negative forces in the invisible world, that connect vibrationally to their own unprocessed astral states of aversion and desire and which can exacerbate trauma.

Conclusion

Western shamanism is a hybrid process taken from indigenous shamanic practices and grafted onto contemporary western culture in the hope of providing a personal-growth pathway that mediates the visible and invisible worlds, the earth and the heavens, the human and the non-human. At its most inadequate, this personal-growth pathway is fraught with the inexperienced practitioner's lack of awareness of the full implications of the invisible powers which they are mediating; processes for which facilitators are often inadequately trained to provide client safety and constructive outcomes. Also, in western culture, they walk a thin line because if spirit possession occurs in facilitators or clients and they cannot exit the experience, they risk being incarcerated in mental health hospitals with a diagnosis of psychosis.

In its best moments as a personal-growth process, the shamanistic pathway provides an experiential pathway to crack western minds out of their enclosed materialistic world-view, expand their consciousness to engage the invisible, the spiritual, the numinous and to re-connect them with the unity of consciousness that pervades all living beings down to the very substance of the earth itself, truly recapturing a respect for Gaia, and a profound recognition of the sacredness of the web of life. It is the blessing of vision captured by Nancy Wood in this excerpt from her poem:

> ... I have seen the world through an eagle's eye
> I have seen if from a gopher's hole
> I have seen the world on fire
> And the sky without a moon.
> All is a circle within me.
> (Nancy Wood, cited in Halifax: pp.137f)

However, it is essential to remember that to have these transpersonal experiences with safety and personal-growth-promoting consequences, one must first have a stable and integrated self, a firm foundation of the autonomous 'I' from which to launch out to the cosmos and to which one can return. People with traumatized or fragmented senses of self, with a weakly developed 'I', with poor boundaries and poor self-delineation may well be hijacked to the sky without a moon, excarnated beyond the soul, into the realms of spirit which engulf such a hapless traveller, ill-prepared to stand in the face of such power and such energetic dissolution and reconstitution. When too much, too soon, of this nature floods the individual, madness rather than illumination is the potential destination.

9. Drugs as pathway

Nothing can bring you peace but yourself
— Ralph Waldo Emerson

Why choose recreational drugs as a pathway to personal growth given the widely publicized health hazards of addiction, the high number of fatalities and the disintegrating lives of long-term addicts? At the heart of the personal-growth approach incorporating recreational drugs is the search for freedom from boredom and a search for meaning. Viktor Frankl (1965) notes that the search for meaning in secular, post-industrial western societies is a core pursuit particularly due to the demise of the church influence. Campbell (2001) notes in his clinical observations of heroin users that their most frequent reference is to boredom, which is typified in statements like: 'If I don't use drugs, I will be bored. I started using because I was bored.' He goes on to note that this chronic boredom often originates in family systems where 'don't feel, don't think, don't speak' are the core messages and that there is the failure by parents to provide a contained, warm, caring space for the growth of children. The family space is empty emotionally and so the boredom arises from a series of empty psychic blackholes within the child, who has no tools to self-soothe and self-resource and, as an adolescent or adult, seeks this sense of feeling and fullness in external stimuli such as drugs. Lievegoed (1990:p.9) notes that in addition to these factors there are also the repressed traumatic experiences that have occurred during childhood which burden and deplete the developing feeling life of the child and, in adolescence, crush or deflect their connection with the world and their ideals. Children that have been abused, violently, sexually or emotionally, may fail to form a connection with the world that is trusting and, in adolescence, may retreat into isolation in the face of their broken trust and woundedness.

There is a wealth of evidence demonstrating that recreational drugs of all types diminish one's consciousness in the present moment. One needs to be fully present in the present moment to be available to oneself and to develop and realize one's full potential. However, culturally the lack of meaning, level of social and personal trauma, and the absence of processes to experience the supra-mundane results in many people, trying to seek a way out. Van der Haar summarizes the dilemma:

> On the one hand a need is apparent in modern man
> (sic) to get to know himself; on the other hand, our
> culture appears to be full of opportunities to turn away
> from oneself, to become addicted to the means of
> diminishing one's consciousness.
> (Van der Haar, 1990:p.7)

The vast majority of hard drug use commences between the ages of seventeen and eighteen when, developmentally, the individual personality is born into the world. Van der Haar elaborates:

> ... the fear of getting to know the world and the self
> ('I') through ones own powers begins to manifest
> itself. The fear is real enough when up bringing

and education have failed to provide the necessary foundations on which to base the shaping of one's own life. (Van der Haar, 1990:p.8)

Furthermore, the permeability of both the first and second thresholds is increasing and more and more adolescents are being confronted with their contents. By permeability I mean the vibrational opaqueness of the thresholds, which traditionally have made it difficult for people to pass across them. Defence mechanisms of denial, sublimation, projection, no longer work well to strengthen the opaqueness of the thresholds and more and more people feel strongly the echoes of their experiences beyond the first threshold, even if they cannot name them. They have feelings of disquiet, general unhappiness, generalized anxiety or the sense that something is not quite right. In passing the first threshold they encounter the first guardian who represents all of a person's shadows with the associated and frightening guilt, shame, self-hatred and low self-esteem. Drugs become a way out of confronting the inner shadow. (Schaik,1990). I would have to confirm this observation on the basis of my clinical work with adolescents, many of whom are now able to see into the interior, invisible dimensions of their experiences whether defined as cellular memories, intergenerational coding or past lives. They are often overwhelmed by what they can observe of their interior experiences, and develop on overwhelming sense of shame and self-contempt unless given appropriate tools to digest the experiences and transform them into self-forgiveness and self-esteem.

Then there is the encounter with the second threshold that they may glimpse in their first drug experiences, which is seductive in the extreme for the bored adolescent with little sense of self-worth or destiny. At the crossing of the second threshold, the path to the macrocosm, they behold the great guardian who is symbolic of their highest potential. Here, in the place of ineffable light, they are blinded by their own potential glory, an experience so exalted and removed from the limitations of day-to-day life that it promises another more exalted experience of life where happiness will be greater. Yet at the same time this becomes a realm where one is unprepared for the paralyzing fear and terror of the magnitude of the forms and forces that exist there (Lievegoed, 1985). Many of the renowned psychiatrist Stanislaw Grof's clients' paintings of their LSD trips capture these macrocosmic states of expansiveness and the uncontrollable blinding forces of light, sound, colour and warmth.

Drugs are substances or compounds used deliberately because they bring about a change in consciousness, usually either a sense of being more hyperactive in the world, that is, 'uppers' such as cocaine, ice, amphetamines, or they bring a sense of being calmer, more relaxed and more in touch with the cosmos through, that is, 'downers' like marihuana, heroin and LSD. Some drugs may provide both upper and downer moments of consciousness. Translated into the anthroposophical growth model, in essence drugs enable the user to force their way through from the material world of lower states of consciousness to the invisible world of higher states of consciousness, and to penetrate both the first threshold and the second thresholds.

Different drugs provide different experiences depending on how they affect the natural protective, energetic, construction of the parts that constitute body, soul and spirit. Dunselman (1993) notes the epidemic in recreational drug use, with a projected growth by 2100 of the number of users exceeding the number of non-users in post-industrial economies. This trend continues when adolescents and adults choose a range of drugs as their personal-growth pathway, because the drugs give them a way of penetrating the layers within body, soul and spirit and enable them to gain particular types of experiences from which they otherwise feel cut off.

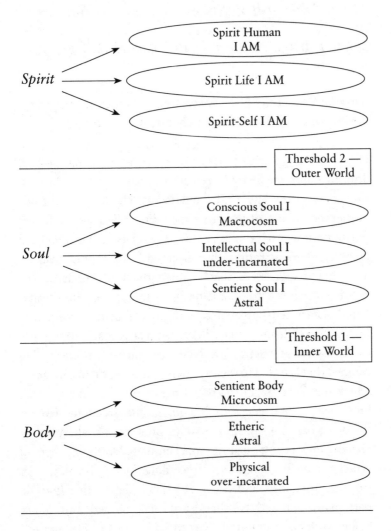

The diagram presented here provides a foundation for the following discussion on the effects of different types of drugs on different parts of a human being, in relation to the two thresholds discussed previously.

The promised benefits and costs of commonly chosen drugs in the pursuit of personal growth.

'Downers' such as LSD, mescaline, psilocybin, magic mushrooms, and associated chemical compounds

LSD was popularized as a therapeutic personal-growth drug by Timothy Leary, a research psychologist at Harvard University in the late 1950s and 1960s. He conducted trials of therapeutic use of the drugs including a behaviour change rehabilitation programme at the Massachusetts Correctional Institute demonstrating that users acquired new insights into their experiences that enabled them to break out of self-defeating and traumatizing behavioural patterns (Leary, 1965). Leary led personal-growth groups in the 1960s and 1970s with colleagues like Allpert, who later assumed the title of Ram Dass as part of the New Age guru phenomena. He claimed that LSD led to the experience of cosmic consciousness which freed one from the social prescriptions and roles that limit one's experiences of happiness and freedom. Use of the drug, particularly among youth populations where Leary also became a drug guru figure, eventually led to widespread criticisms of its side-effects including health breakdowns, suicides, psychosis and other associated destructive lifestyle patterns which led to the drug been banned and Leary being widely discredited (Greenfield, 2006). He himself was eventually imprisoned for drug trafficking and began to believe that he was a reincarnation of Jesus Christ, an outcome of a fractured second threshold which left him with delusions of grandeur drawn from images beyond the second threshold.

Metzner (2005:p.25) distinguishes between hallucinogenic or psychedelic drugs, which he argues are consciousness-expanding, and drugs such as opiates, alcohol, cocaine and amphetamines, which lead to fixated and contracted states of consciousness. He cites programmes conducted in the treatment of alcoholics with LSD by Osmond and documented by Passie (1985) which propose that one or a small number of high dose sessions would release the unconscious mind in the form of a vivid hallucinatory imagery which would lead to insight and potential transformation. He goes on to argue that Native Americans involved in Peyote rituals of the Native American Church have been consistently successful in alcoholism recovery, and cites the works of McClusky (1997) and Horgan (2003). He also cites Delgado and Mereno's (1998) comparatively successful trials of LSD with obsessive-compulsive disorders.

Metzner (2005) concludes that it is essential that such therapeutic interventions involve a supportive therapeutic setting and community, prolonged guided experience of self-confrontation and the acceptance and support of like-minded individuals. He notes that other cognitive processes such as mindfulness meditation can be used to achieve the same effect of counteracting fixations and attachments. In relation to the consequences for the whole human being of taking the psychedelic drug approach versus 'mindfulness' there is no doubt that the 'mindfulness meditation' approach is much healthier physically, emotionally and mentally. It does not have the profound costs of the psychedelic drug approach and it develops the individual's 'I' as the locus of control over their life and experiences. This is much more preferable in terms of the development of an individual's health rather than bypassing the individual's 'I', which is weakening for the development of individual will, focus and self-integration.

Psychedelic drugs cause an artificial, partial split between the physical body and the etheric body. This causes the etheric forces to become free and enter the astral body where the memories of all our experiences are stored. These memories start to be loosened so that we have perceptions of things long forgotten or repressed. This is akin to the process that happens in near-death experiences when a person recalls reviewing their life experiences as if in a reverse video tape. This drug particularly affects the liver and kidneys, both of which are organs that store intense emotional experiences, particularly fear (Dunselman, 1990:p.46). The etheric body is a body of light and energy, and when detached from the physical body can enter other areas of soul consciousness and cause intense colour and light psychedelic experiences. However, since the astral areas of experience which contain the conscious awareness are now mismatched with the etheric and physical bodies, as a result of this forced split, so time and space dimensions are distorted. This is illustrated by LSD users allowing themselves to receive third-degree burns while on the beach without any awareness of the length of time they have been exposed to the sun, and without any awareness of bodily discomfort. The etheric is forced to float away to the universe from where it originates leaving the user in a dissolution process, so that no personal growth can occur. In fact, the contrary occurs as more and more energy has to be invested in the physical breakdown of the body as physical health cannot be maintained without a vibrant etheric or life body (Dunselman: 1993:p.52).

'Uppers', such as speed, amphetamines, ice, cocaine, crack and other associated chemical compounds

These drugs force the astral body into the physical body as a result of a loosened etheric and this releases excessive energy into the limbs and the thinking, which enables takers of this drug to excel at sports, physical activities and other activities requiring considerable energy. An excess of will forces are released so that the person feels invincible. Feelings of vulnerability, doubt, insecurity, fear, doubt, low self-esteem disappear. In the words of Freud, himself a cocaine user: 'You are full of vitality and the will to work ... you can perform long and intense mental or physical tasks without a trace of fatigue' (Dunselman,1993:p.213). The costs of intense and prolonged drug use are substantial including the breakdown of the physical body, extreme tiredness, lethargy, depression and, in some cases, suicidal ideation, paranoid fears and tactile hallucinations. Users may report insects, snakes crawling over their body or other creepy crawlies under their skin. Finally, psychosis can occur and will often incorporate a persecution complex and visual hallucinations because of the fracturing of the threshold and the ungoverned flooding of the consciousness with material previously inaccessible or held behind defence mechanisms. In the words of Ibsen, 'humankind can bear very little reality' at one time. Such drugs overload the capacity of the conscious mind, or the astrality, to digest and integrate the material that is released by the drugs.

Marijuana, opium and heroin

These drugs, although of different chemical compositions, are considered together because they have a similar effect on the human being's constitution. They create a gap, not just between the physical and etheric body, but also between the etheric and the astral body, which forces the astral or soul body of the individual outwards artificially into the invisible world of feeling creating a dreamy consciousness which Steiner describes in relation to opium:

> ... (the addict) enjoys feelings of sweetness: this is very agreeable . It is as if the etheric body is permeated with sugar, a special kind of sugar, sweet through and through. At the same time the astral body is free from the material body, and allows (the user) to observe everything but in a distinct way. (Dunselman, 1990:p.51)

Literally, the user loses touch with reality. The cost is that in between trips, the 'I' is so excarnated, or pushed out of the body, that life is experienced as 'grey and dull', the will forces are weakened and the emotional life of joy and sorrow disappears into a wooden type of emotional life, dried out and foggy (Dunselman, 1990:p.52). Worse still, the over-expanded etheric force often collapses like a tired old balloon that has been over-inflated. At that point the astral experiences flood the user and they become psychotic, unable to digest what arises. With heroin, the effects are more intense for not only is the physical body poisoned but the 'I' is also forced so far out of the astral that inner growth comes to a halt. It expels all feelings leaving only intellectual thinking and a desiccated human soul.

Characteristics of Healthy Personal growth

1. Promotes the growth of autonomous 'I'

The coming to maturity of the integrated self or 'I' is a process occurring over a period of twenty-eight years. Drugs, particularly in adolescence hijack the growth of the autonomous 'I' which is replaced by what Steiner termed the: 'Oppositional "I"' and what Sherwood (2007:p.260–63) describes as the thought form or 'essence' of the addictive substance. It takes on an oppositional stance to the growth of the user. It is very difficult to kick a drug habit prior to twenty-one years of age because the client's 'I' is not sufficiently developed, or incarnated into the persona to overcome the power of the 'oppositional "I"'. Therefore, addictive substances all retard the growth of the autonomous 'I' and weaken its growth process (Lelieveld, 1990).

2. Emphasizes the client's capacity as initiator of processes

Drug use overrides the user's 'I' so that the drugs start to direct the user's life and the 'oppositional "I"' or essence of the substance occupies the place in the user's soul of their own 'I'. Once the user is addicted, their capacity to initiate change is very limited. In fact, developmentally, if a fourteen year old becomes a serious addict and remains so until twenty-eight years of age, their growth is arrested at the fourteen-year-old level in their soul, even though physically they are twenty-eight years of age. Drugs literally bypass the user's 'I' and recovery from addiction requires one to go back to the arrested level and undergo the developmental tasks of that level (Dunselman, 1990).

3. Provides processes so client can sustain improvements

Despite providing initial feelings of personal growth, such as increased awareness or insight, increased emotional energy, richer and more diverse human experiences, drugs are profoundly misleading. By the time the client is addicted, the personal-growth process has turned into a physically, etherically, emotionally and spiritually destructive process; the precise nature depending on how the particular drug creates gaps between the different sheaths or components of the human constitution; for example, gaps between the etheric and astral sheath with LSD.

4. Monitors the client to ensure their 'I' can digest and integrate the experiences

Drug addiction leaves the user's sheaths so damaged that, in many cases, they cannot be entirely reconstituted. So, for example, heavy marijuana users may have so damaged the sheaths between the etheric and astral body that they are prone to emotional flooding even after they have given up the addiction. The first threshold no longer acts effectively as a barrier between the inner content of all of our experiences and daily life.

Case study

Don had a troubled childhood with his father leaving the family when he was eight years old and his mother remarrying a violent man who thrashed Don and his brothers for no predictable reason. Don had to work long hours on the family farm and schooling was disparaged by his stepfather. When Don was fourteen he was introduced to marijuana by some mates when he was discussing how much he hated his stepfather, and how depressed he became when he saw his mother and brothers beaten repeatedly. He felt powerless, useless and overwhelmed by the problems in his own life and in his family. He wanted to be a sheet-metal worker but his stepfather ridiculed him, saying he had only the ability to be a rubbish collector. Don found that marijuana gave him a sense of release from all of these burdens of his unhappy life and left him feeling content, happy and blissfully unconcerned with the day-to-day issues of his life. It was time-out in a world that was worth living in; a reality that was worth knowing.

Don began to see marijuana as a way of connecting up with the cosmos, of developing a sense of connectedness beyond himself. Don's habit developed over his teenage years and eventually, at sixteen, he found work as a farmhand. At that stage, he left home and went interstate seeking a life away from his family and hoping for better things. He was a regular smoker, especially after work and at the weekends. He was a tall slender, sensitive man and described himself as socially lacking in confidence. However, by the age of twenty-five he met and married an eighteen-year-old girl with whom he was to have three children over the next six years. Don continued to work as a labourer with low wages and the household budget was always pressured. His dope smoking continued, much to the annoyance of his partner, who complained that it made him unavailable to the relationship. She also saw it as creating a large hole in the family budget and she grew increasingly unhappy. One day he arrived home from work and she was gone with the three-, four- and five-year-old children, who he never saw again.

Don became very depressed. By this time he was thirty-one years of age and his dope-smoking habit escalated. He began to organize his life around accessing and smoking dope rather than organizing dope smoking around his life. Eventually, he met a lovely girl called Sam but who was also a heavy user of marijuana. They become a couple and organized their lives around procuring and smoking dope. By this stage, both were unemployed and relying on unemployment benefits to eat and to buy marijuana. They were also squatting in an abandoned farmhouse without electricity, sewerage or running water.

Don's friends now were mostly dope smokers. After a series of infections, Don became physically run down. He was now thirty-seven but his health was deteriorating as he ate irregularly and avoided any medical services. He had acquired a new supplier of marijuana and had settled into a trip which he says went badly wrong. Firstly, he became quite paranoid, feeling that the local authorities were out to get him and incarcerate him in prison in the inhospitable reaches of the country. He began to believe that it was part of a grand plot to kill him. He did not remember the details of this experience but his partner explained that he became increasingly agitated, removed most of his clothes so he would not be identified and ran off into the state forest to evade the people coming to imprison him. She was unable to persuade him otherwise and soon lost track of him in the forest when night fell and she decided to return home. Don did not return home and twenty-four hours later she notified the police that he was a missing person. She was particularly concerned because it was winter and cold. Forty-eight hours later Don was found wandering half-naked down a major highway, with arms flailing in the air, trying to wave down a lift from passers-by without success. Don resisted arrest, accused the police of being members of the government that was spying on him. And accused them of having taken his children away and of having imprisoned them.

However, in his weakened condition he was easily arrested by the police and admitted to the local mental health hospital. His body was covered with scratches and bruises and streaked with dry blood. He informed the nurses and doctors that he would not take anything they prescribed him as he was into natural remedies. After five days in the hospital he left without advising anyone by walking out of the hospital premises and heading back to the forest. By this stage, he was no longer psychotic but bent on escape from the hospital system which he detested. He walked ten kilometres under the cover of the forest to a friend's place and asked if he could remain there while he recovered. The hospital staff either did not notice his departure or were relieved he had left, but did not report it. His partner knew nothing about it, but discovered it a week later when she went to visit him. Meanwhile, Don was still certain that marijuana was a pathway to freedom from pain and lacked insight into the consequences of his addiction, especially as he had a strong resolve to remain away from the authorities and the hospital system. His friend convinced him to come to counselling with hopes that he might gain insight into his problem. Don had now been a heavy marijuana user for twenty years.

Although I was able to give Don insight into the connection between heavy marijuana use and psychosis, as a result of the collapse of the etheric body, Don was certain that if he could recover his physical health and well-being, he would not be vulnerable to psychotic attacks again. He was not willing to work on the emotional abuse and abandonment that vibrated in every cell of his body, and which were numbed by his marijuana habit. As he explained: 'Marijuana is the only thing that gives me a feeling that my life is manageable and not overwhelming.' I understood the pain of this man's life story and although his choice to continue was not skilful in my view, my heart understood a man's desperation to stay away from the fragments of his own shattered heart.

Summary of the outcomes of healthy and unhealthy personal growth

1. I am more present in my daily life

Drugs like marijuana in Don's case, did not support him being more present to his life or more able to deal with the challenges in his life. Rather it gave him another worldly focus and became an escape from his present daily life. To the degree in which drugs remove a person's capacity to deal with their daily life, do they lose their sense of focus. Their will to change is extremely weakened. Van Gerven (1990:p.3) describes addiction as, 'an attack on the ability to live one's own life'. Drugs accelerate the catabolic breakdown processes in the human body, by artificially separating out the etheric body from the physical body and the astral body, and by poisoning many of the vital organs of the body, so that over the course of addiction the person's physical health fails in varying degrees. De Alba et al (2005) noted that 45% of drug users, who were admitted to an urban detoxification unit in the USA, had chronic illness and 80% had prior hospitalizations, even though the mean age was only thirty-five years. They had a far greater rate of physical illnesses than a comparative age and gender group in the population that was not engaged in drug abuse behaviour. The range of breakdown illnesses resulting from drug abuse include: cardiovascular disease, strokes, cancer, liver and lung diseases, kidney damage and neurological damage. (http;//

www.nida.nih.gov/consequences/) Mertens et al (2003) found that one-third of medical conditions examined were more common among substance abusers than among people who did not use drugs.

2. I am empowered to shape my destiny

Addiction erodes the individual's capacity to direct their life's experiences and the sense of self becomes increasingly weakened and fragmented. This is because the 'I' or higher self of the individual which is capable of insight, focus and will is forced out of the body by the drugs repeatedly weakening the individual's ability to act with an integrated self in their day-to-day life, and to bring insight, focus and motivation to deal with day-to-day challenges. In order to free the individual, so they can be in control of their own destiny again, something needs to re-kindle and ignite the spark of their 'I'. Sometimes a life change such as the death of a friend, exhaustion with the lifestyle, or a pregnancy may do this. A supportive therapeutic community can act in place of the individual's 'I' during a transition phase while the 'I' is recovering and becoming present again in the person's body, so they may begin to direct their lives. (Van Gerven, 1990:p.3)

3. I am increasingly free from reactions

In addiction, the pre- and post-drug intervals that punctuate the individual's life demonstrate an intensity of negative reactive feelings, depending on the type of drug used. So, for example, with cocaine use there is likely to be a paranoid type of aggression, while with marijuana use, there is likely to be a dullness of being, a vague emptiness, a sense of loss or fearful flashbacks.

4. I am more fully who I am: 'self-actualization' and 'self-transcendence'

Leary praised drugs, particularly LSD, as the best pathways to developing one's unique potential, and to dissolving psychological blocks and defence mechanisms. He argued that only on drugs like LSD can one truly be free to be oneself and to simultaneously experience ever greater transcendent experiences, which link one with the cosmos. This may be the experience of the early stages of drug usage. However, this comes at an extremely high cost which ultimately results in the loss of who you are as a unique person, and increasing isolation and often paranoia from the world of connectedness. It is the personal growth path of the poisoned apple. It may taste fine initially but then one slowly dies of the addictive poison which destroys body, soul and spirit. Dunselman describes the delusion of this path by citing an opium addict's description:

> The first time is a dream, an unbelievable experience
> of paradise, an encounter with the gods. The first few
> times are beautiful, so that you are reconciled with
> your existence. You are able to forgive and at last you
> can breathe deeply and freely again ... it's not long
> that the day comes when a triple dose no longer has
> any effect ... everything is reversed. It's only when you
> don't take anything that you notice anything — all
> the pain and misery that is in the world. From that
> moment you pay a high price to feel normal. You
> suffer merely to avoid suffering. You run from one
> place to another, stealing, hustling, buying, chased
> by the police, and constantly ripped off by dealers ...
> (Dunselman, 1993:p.15)

Furthermore, as Lievegoed notes, drugs that drive out the astral body and leave the etheric body have risks of possession by an alien consciousnesses:

An unattended ether(ic) body attracts elemental beings: one takes one's chances at what comes in then. One gains the impressions that for opium these are luciferic beings, while for LSD and the Mexican poisons they are ahrimanic beings ... what these beings do in the ether(ic) body one finds out upon return of the spirit-soul being ('I'), in the hangover ... (Lievegoed, 1984:p.199)

With drugs, astral experience can be unleashed unpredictably and randomly which is an experience described by drug users as a 'bad trip', where they become suicidal, homicidal, fearful or terrified and unable to control their behaviour. Timothy Leary's LSD drug-addicted daughter attempted to murder her son and her lover and then committed suicide by jumping out of a high-rise building.

The holistic model of personal growth for body, soul and spirit: The consequences

Initially, addiction begins either because the 'I' feels too weak to encounter the forces it experiences in its personal, family and community life or because the 'I' feels unable to connect to some-thing that is meaningful, that arouses the sense of vision and purpose fundamental to the 'I'. However, once the 'I' is part of the addictive cycle its power to control the process is eroded. Sherwood (2007:p.257) conducted a phenomenological piece of research on clients experiencing addictive behaviours. Whenever clients were asked to enter their bodies at the point of craving, the following patterns of experience were found. These are:

a. client's experience their 'I' leaving during the moments of craving;

b. clients experience an implant in their bodies at the point of craving which they feel has been placed there by something, or someone other than themselves;

c. clients experience an attachment or cord leading from the implant to the essence of the addictive substance which client's draw and which Steiner termed the 'oppositional "I"';

d. This oppositional 'I' drives the craving for the addictive substance and stands over the client's 'I' with threats of suffering and pain to the client if the craved for substance is not ingested;

e. clients experience a pattern of traumatic imprints under the implant which relate to incidents in their earlier life. In order to deal with the underlying experiential traumas, which hold the implant in place, it is necessary to undertake energetically based therapy; one form of which is exemplified in Sherwood (2007), which provides processes for transforming these patterns of woundedness, whether as a result of active or passive abuse, into sites of well-being and flourishing mental health.

In order to free the client from the 'oppositional "I"' and to rebuild the client's 'I', it is essential that a rigorous programme of re-parenting the 'I' is followed. Vogt (2002:p.89–93) outlines this process which involves literally going over the biography of the client in seven-year phases, starting with birth and providing environmental support in a therapeutic community like ARTA for the client which is appropriate to each phase of the biography being worked with. So, for example, when the client is in the 0–7 phase, the environment will be warm, nurturing, with lots of imaginative and physical activities and very little responsibility. Literally, the incarnation process from babyhood to adulthood is re-run in the therapeutic community of ARTA which has a success rate of 85% and is one of the most effective drug rehabilitation programmes in Europe (Van Den Berg (ed.), 1990).

Drugs, other than downers, make people less available to their daily lives. While drugs like cocaine increase people's performance in the physical world, increase their endurance and stamina in the short-term but, in the long-term, this is not sustainable and extreme exhaustion, depression and moodiness prevail. This is due to the lack of 'I' presence directing the integration process and an excess of astral activity in the case of cocaine which bypasses the 'I' and the feeling life to produce hardening in the thinking and willing of an individual, often at great personal and social cost. Drugs chemically distort this balance in different ways. Thinking is overstimulated by cocaine and speed, while LSD and mescaline produce altered perceptions and inner imagery in the mind. Marijuana intensifies feelings, particularly happy moods, sweet dreams and relaxed feelings, while heroin and opiates produce a flash of euphoria and a dulling of the sensations of fear, sorrow, pain and shame, and reduce consciousness of feelings to a general sense of well-being. Cocaine acts particularly on the will, stimulating it so that people can perform physical, sexual and mental feats well beyond their normal motivation (Dunselman 1993:pp.32f).

Thus, it is clear that drugs can separate out the forces of the human being and place one force only in the foreground. While independent control over these forces is a sign of advanced spiritual growth in this model, and a preparedness to cross the second threshold, in the case of drugs, the self is weakened. In its place are the drugs that direct the process of separation beyond the control of the 'I'. Furthermore, as the 'I' weakens with continued drug use the ability to integrate these three disappears and the person lives out of the one-sided faculty promoted by their particular drug addiction, that is, thinking, feeling or willing. Some people try to counter this imbalance by taking uppers and downers, such as Ecstasy, which have a wide range of debilitating after-effects depending on frequency of usage.

Conclusion

In working with drugs as a pathway to personal growth, the illusionary nature of the promise has been exposed many times to those with addictive behaviours. However, the task for the personal-growth pathway in light of the holistic model is to strengthen the 'I', the spirit of the human manifest in the soul and the body that can stand for hope amid despairing circumstances; that can see light in the darkness; and that can find vision among the ashes of dreams. As Vogt points out:

> It isn't a question of battling against drugs,
> But of fighting for:
> The individual who has overcome them.
> (Vogt, 2002:p.17)

10. Meditation as pathway

Awareness gives you your life back. You can then
decide what to do with it.
— Kabat Zinn

Meditation as a pathway to personal growth has gained
widespread appeal in western countries in recent years,
particularly as eastern religious traditions such as Buddhism
and Hinduism have become global. An ancient and well-
proven pathway to personal growth in the east, meditation
is having major impacts on the personal-growth industry
in the west. It is estimated that there are ten million
meditation practitioners in the US and it is now one of the
most widely practised, enduring and researched pathways
to personal growth and mental well-being (Deurr, 2004).
In Australia, the number of Buddhist organizations has
risen from three in 1972 to over 400 in 2008, which is
typical of trends across the western world. The popularity
of meditation has been largely due to the desire for
techniques to relieve stress, create peace of mind, increase
quality of life in the present moment, and experience
more connectedness with self, others and the community
in compassionate and heartfelt ways (Sherwood, 2004).
Meditation is a term used to refer to a variety of self-
directed and self-regulating processes:

that focus on training attention and awareness in order
to bring mental processes under greater voluntary
control and thereby foster general mental well-being and
growth and/or specific capacities such as calm, clarity and
concentration (Walsh & Shapiro, 2006:pp.228f)

There are many different types of meditation practice
but Goleman establishes two main categories: concentration
methods (transcendental meditation/TM) and insight
techniques (Vipassna). Tibetan tradition would also add
analytical meditation processes whereby the person focuses
on an image such as that of a great spiritual being. In the
concentration methods there is a focus on inner states,
such as breath, which by restricting attention to one point,
calm the ordinary mental chatter and induce states of calm
and peacefulness characterized by quiet and tranquillity. By
contrast, insight meditation practices, of which Kabat Zinn's
(2005) mindfulness is a good example, focus the attention on
the nature of thoughts, feelings, and observe them skilfully
in their arising and passing away without attachment or
judgment of one self, or one's mind. The aim is to become
more fully present in the present moment and not become
attached to even equanimity of mind. As Bogart (1991)
indicates in his work, different types of meditation styles
are associated with different patterns of brain activity. It is
important to select the correct type to match one's particular
personal-growth or therapeutic goal. In addition, increasing
research has been done on mindfulness-based cognitive
therapy establishing the effectiveness of this combination of
meditation and cognitively based therapy. Meadows' (2004)
randomized control trial of mindfulness-based cognitive
therapy for the prevention of relapse and recurrence of
depression is a case in point.

The promised benefits

The benefits of meditation as a pathway to personal growth, which encompasses flourishing mental health, are most impressive. It is one of the most thoroughly researched and validated processes. Research shows that meditation can improve a variety of psychological and physical health issues. Murphy and Donavan (1997) note that it improves stuttering, asthma and hormonal disorders including type 2 diabetes and pre-menstrual syndrome. There is extensive research showing the benefits of meditation in reducing distress in cancer patients, and in reducing hypertension and hypercholesterolemia, (Walsh & Shapiro, 2006). Mindfulness practice enhances one's depth of perception, levels of empathy, concentration, focus, attention to detail and learning ability. Shure et al (2008) noted that counselling students, who had been taught mindfulness meditation practice, reported positive physical, emotional, mental, spiritual and interpersonal changes, as well as substantial beneficial effects on their counselling skills and therapeutic relationships. Hawkins (2003) noted that TM reduces substance abuse, as well as anxiety, depression and other forms of psychological distress. He noted that over thirty-nine research studies have been conducted on the rehabilitative effects of TM on youths at risk, prisoners and addicts, and the results have been most positive in terms of increasing participants' skilful behaviour. In particular, prisoners show rapid positive change in risk factors associated with criminal behaviour, including anxiety, aggression, hostility, moral judgement and substance abuse.

As a consequence of extraordinary numbers of research projects confirming the positive mental benefits of meditation practices, meditation centres are flourishing. Kabat Zinn, the world's leading mindfulness meditation exponent describes in his book, Full Catastrophe Living, how simple mindfulness meditation techniques can facilitate people overcoming physical and emotional pain or shock. Kabat Zinn summarizes the personal-growth power of mindfulness meditation which provides a:

> powerful route for getting ourselves unstuck, back
> into touch with our own wisdom and vitality. It is a
> way to take charge of the direction and quality of our
> own lives, including our relationship within the family,
> our relationship to work, and to the larger world and
> planet, and most fundamentally, your relationship with
> yourself as a person. (Kabat Zinn, 2005:p.5)

The Hidden costs

Meditation practices have been thoroughly researched and, to date, there is little evidence of adverse reactions of people using meditation. Where there are adverse reactions, it is usually in relation to boundary breaches from meditation teachers who have become self-styled gurus, or who have unresolved personal issues which they project onto the meditation students. In his research, Kornfield (1988) noted two major problems in over twenty meditation centres in the United States. These were unresolved, personal, relational and vocational issues that meditation practices have not altered and major upheavals around the meditation teacher in relation to power, sex, money and intoxicants. Rubin, (1996) notes the dangers of such unethical positions, enabling some practitioners to rationalize away their personal responsibility for their behaviour in light of their illusionary notion of self.

Another hidden hazard can occur for certain people with serious mental health histories who undertake too much meditation. They can become so seriously flooded by what arises from across the first threshold, in terms of their unintegrated traumatic experiences and shadow states, that it may trigger a mental health collapse. Long meditation retreats are not recommended for such people and experienced retreat facilitators request that people with such a mental health history do not undertake long mediations, that is, of more than 2–3 days.

Although personal growth with well-conducted meditation can be experienced as slow, it is most often sustainable and has no inner cost. Meditation practices are high on sustainability and provide a pace at which the new insights are integrated through the flow of the breathing and the resultant greater presence to day-to-day activities when practised accurately and with focus. Occasionally, some people use sitting meditation as a process of becoming less present to their daily problems by focusing on the breath and on 'floating away into some bliss-like state', which is not transferrable to their day-to-day life. Effective meditation done accurately should increase one's day-to-day presence in the world and assist the person to be less accident-prone, less forgetful and more present in one's body.

Characteristics of Healthy Personal growth

1. Promotes the growth of autonomous 'I'

Meditation practices conducted by the individual empower the individual with the capacity to take control of experiences that otherwise seem unavoidable, while releasing them from

over-attachment to outcomes. Epstein describes the process
of meditation as creating bare attention to our experiences:

> Bare attention ... facilitates the ability to transform
> psychic disturbances into objects of meditation turning
> the proverbial threat into a challenge and is, therefore,
> of immense psychotherapeutic benefit. There is
> no emotional experience, no mental event, and no
> disavowed or estranged aspect of ourselves that cannot
> be worked with, through the strategy of bare attention.
> (Epstein, 1995:p.127)

If one learns to meditate and relax methodically week after
week, by attending good quality mediation programmes,
one learns to master the process of beginning to meditate,
arriving at the relaxed state and gradually learns to maintain
it in more and more in challenging conditions in day-to-day
life. It is like building up the muscles of one's higher mind;
the place of insight which is at the heart of the integrated
self or 'I' and feels able to originate changes as required
to optimize one's quality of life. Thich Naht Hanh (1987)
and Kabat Zinn (1990) illustrate personal-growth processes
within meditation practice that support the characteristics of
healthy personal growth.

2. Emphasizes the client's capacity as initiator of processes

At the heart of healthy personal growth is the sense of
the person initiating changes that support their growth.
Meditation practice does exactly that, giving the client
tools so they can initiate and manage the quality of their
own life on a daily basis. Many of the accolades directed
at mindfulness practice by physicians and psychotherapists
are based upon meditation's capacity to enhance the client's

self-control and personal mastery over their own mental and physical states of experience:

> Despite the spectacular advances in medical science in the 20th century our patients continue to struggle with stress, pain and illness. Jon Kabat Zinn has added the critical ingredient to our therapeutic armanentarum, self-control. (Dr Dalem, cited in Kabat Zinn, 1990)

Meditation strategies, once learnt, are highly portable and can be practised in many locations, at the client's initiation and at no cost.

3. Provides processes so client can sustain improvements

Mediative strategies that are self-directed can be transferred to a variety of situations and self-initiated at moments of need. Bogart (1991) cites Delmonte's work on clients who practise meditation to show that they consistently score highly in terms of self-esteem, self-concept and self-actualization, which all indicate incremental and sustainable personal growth.

4. Monitors the client to ensure their 'I' can digest and integrate the experiences

The human being's natural rhythms occur when a person is breathing fully. When we are stressed, threatened or fearful we restrict our breathing and breathe shallowly. The breathing rhythm slows down not speeds up, as we integrate experiences into ourselves in a natural meditation process. In the slowing down process of restoring the breath, we are able to develop insights into our emotional life and to let go of peripheral emotional and mental noise (Ellison, 2006). In place of quiet and slow rhythmical breathing, we have the ability not only to see our own minds clearly but also to start to free ourselves from enmeshment in other people's minds. We start to develop insight. As Ricard notes: 'You can become familiar with the way emotions arise, how they can either overwhelm your mind or vanish without making an impact' (Ellison, 2006).

Meditation practices are highly skilful means to personal growth, but used inappropriately by people with a serious mental health history, they can go wrong even with the best intentions and highest commitment to one's inner work.

Case study

Tony was thirty years old when he came to therapy looking very underweight, with dark-ringed eyes and lethargy of body and spirit. He only spoke with a tone of enthusiasm when he talked about his meditation practice. Tony talked about his meditation practice for thirty minutes without needing any comments from me. He clearly was passionate about this aspect of his life. In his quest for peace, the nature and cause of his suffering and a way through it all to happiness and freedom from stress, Tony had discovered a meditation group in the next suburb which taught meditation. He was only twenty-two years of age at the time and enjoyed the company of the other meditators and their common goals and aspirations, which were peace of mind and freedom from stress. Tony had been looking for something meaningful for a few years so he grasped this opportunity to become a skilled meditator with both hands.

He practised sitting meditation daily, one hour in the morning and one hour in the evening. He became very devoted to his spiritual meditation teacher and began to take spiritual initiations with him which meant that, in addition to meditation practices, Tony was given special chants to complete daily as these would accelerate his spiritual progress. Tony was a sensitive young man. He described what he termed as 'an episode' following his mother's death when he was eighteen. He stopped eating and eventually developed behaviour which had been labelled as psychotic by the hospital authorities where he had been admitted. He describes the period of his life preceding this event as very stressful, as a result of university exams and his mother's extended illness prior to her death from cancer. After a couple of weeks in hospital and the prescription of certain drugs, Tony returned to his studies at university. He completed them and graduated as a social worker when he was twenty-one.

Tony admits that his boundaries are poor and that he is like a vacuum cleaner for stress in any environment. He describes meditation as a way of feeling he can cope with the world. Tony had been referred to counselling following another recent psychotic breakdown. Tony was somewhat puzzled by this breakdown as he could not identify any particularly stressful circumstance in his life. Quite the contrary, in the weeks prior to the most recent episode in hospital, Tony had been meditating for up to four hours a day and was impressed with how long he could meditate. He first began to notice he was not feeling grounded during a ten-day meditation retreat he had undertaken. This was the first long meditation retreat he had undertaken in his life. During the retreat, he started to observe that at times distressing images would spontaneously arise, some from his early childhood and other distressful images for which he could not identify the source. On returning home after the retreat, he was flooded with traumatic imagery and began to believe that it was part of a UFO plot to destabilize his brain. In fact, he was certain he was the subject of some very dark forces using his brain experimentally.

He became increasingly occupied with tracking down these forces, neglected his normal eating and sleeping routines until he felt so preoccupied with his thoughts that he did not show up for work. After three days of not appearing at work without any phone calls, one of his work colleagues decided to call in on the way home to see how he was doing. She found him at 6pm walking down the middle of the main highway in his pyjamas and shouting to the traffic: 'Stop me. Kill me now.' He told his colleague the dark forces were pressuring him to kill his meditation teacher and, rather than do such a terrible deed, he was going to kill himself so he could not harm his teacher, as he felt he was losing control of his mind. His colleague talked him into accompanying her to the hospital where he was admitted to the psychiatric ward, where he was diagnosed as experiencing a psychotic episode and drugged accordingly.

Tony presented in therapy with a clear wish to minimize the chances of another episode which would result in his re-admission to hospital. He wanted to learn early diagnostic and preventative strategies to stop the recurrence of such an event and he refused to take prescribed medications because the side effects were too unpleasant for him. The most difficult part of the therapy was to convince Tony that long periods of sitting meditation were not beneficial to his constitution. He used long hours of sitting meditation to remain dissociated from the world. This was evident because after meditation practice he was less present to the physical world around him and his day-to-day tasks, than prior to meditation. With the help of his meditation teacher we came to an agreement where Tony would focus primarily on walking meditation, breathing down to the tips of his toes as he walked back and forth on a twenty-five-metre pathway at his home. Sitting meditation was restricted to a maximum of thirty minutes per day.

Tony is a good illustration that large amounts of sitting meditation practice are not usually beneficial for people with a predisposition to serious mental health issues, particularly psychosis (Walsh & Vaughan, 1993; Wilber et al, 1986).

Summary of the outcomes of healthy and unhealthy personal growth

1. I am more present in my daily life
Being present in the present moment is generally a core result of effective meditation practice. One works to fully occupy one's body through breathing fully into all parts of the body and hence releasing blocks to the breath that are a result of emotional and mental trauma. As these blocks are released in the body, the person becomes more fully present in their body. It is essential that the imprints stored in the astrality are released and healed so that the compassion mind may pervade the way that one is in the world, freed from aversion and desire, judgement and self-loathing. Then, upon the firm foundation of the compassion mind, one can integrate intellectual soul or wisdom mind as it is termed in Buddhist practice.

While meditation practice is designed to make people more present to their day-to-day lives, for some people it is an opportunity to further anchor themselves in the upper pole of thinking and to remain detached from willing or feeling. Tony is such an example. Such people inadvertently use meditation as a process to 'escape' from the world and the realities of their life. Correct meditation practice leads one to greater awareness of life and more effective functioning as one develops strategic depth so that one is not overwhelmed by feelings, but rather can skilfully choose how to live without being driven by reactions and projections. To prevent the dissociation experienced by Tony, walking meditation can be helpful because it requires one to focus attention on the breath and the feet simultaneously and effectively 'grounds' the person.

Both insight and concentration methods of meditation work to increase awareness and, through that awareness, work to increase skilful actions in day-to-day life. Sherwood (2004) cites how awakening through meditation practice leads to social transformations in education, the environment, the peace movement, social services and health care. Queen summarizes it as follows:

> Once there is seeing, there must be acting
> We must be aware of the real problems of the world.
> Then with mindfulness, we will know what to do
> And what not to do, to be of help. (Queen, 2000:p.5)

2. I am empowered to shape my destiny

Through meditation processes the person comes to be the initiator of change because they come to apprehend their experiences directly, so that they can, in Elwood's terms, 'speak from their experience rather than about their experience.' (1983:p.44) This process of meditation assists the person to go beneath their familiar responses to a particular situation, to contact the fresh immediate quality in the experience unmasked by the coloured reactions of life. Here, the individual experiences the capacity not only to see things afresh but also to become aware of the choices of how to be in their life differently. Rather than feeling a victim of circumstances, one becomes very aware that all states of response belong to oneself, and can be changed directly by the way one changes one's mind. This is a very empowering realization and breaks us out of the futile cycle of blaming others for our unhappiness, or waiting for others to change so we can feel happy and fulfilled.

3. I am increasingly free from reactions

Cornfield (1988) and Epstein (1996) note that many wounded adults in western societies are called to meditation as a way of dealing with their distress, that is largely a result of childhood neglect and family trauma. Like Tony, they have deeply traumatized backgrounds that have resulted in a fragmented sense of self, low self-esteem and many repressed fears. Cornfield and Epstein both argue that meditation should not be seen as a panacea for these people and should be combined with skilful psychotherapy. While meditation can provide tools to assist people to reduce these turbulent states of mind, it does not address in all cases, the deeper fragmentation of self underlying these emotional states in some individuals.

However, meditation practices are most effective in creating bodily and mental awareness so as to assist people to identify how much bodily distress is the result of unnecessary mental states of attachment, aversion, desire and anger. Kabat Zinn (1993:p.27) emphasizes the importance of using meditation with bodily awareness to create freedom from such unnecessary states of suffering.

4. I am more fully who I am: 'self-actualization' and 'self-transcendence'

Meditation practices in particular value and develop transpersonal states of experience that go beyond the individual self; what is sometimes referred to as 'non-self' or 'inter-being', that results from a skilful crossing of the second threshold. Meditation practices offer a rigorous framework of growth to prepare for these higher states and to gradually develop them through consistent inner practice. This facilitates the movement to transpersonal states so that the individual has ownership over the process and which builds upon the individual's developed self. It is recognised that the movement to self-transcendence takes considerable inner growth and rigorous practice of mind.

The holistic model of personal growth for body, soul and spirit: the consequences

In Buddhist meditation practice, it is critical that the individual takes responsibility for applying the processes regularly to their state of mind so that they may experience the benefit of what, in the anthropsophical model, would be termed the integrated 'I'. In meditative traditions, this would usually be termed the place of insight, or higher mind, in contrast to day-to-day mind or ordinary mind that is caught up in the web of delusion, ignorance and desire. In skilful meditation practice, where a person is not seriously traumatized or has a very fragile sense of self-esteem, meditation practices tend to lead to controlled processes for exploring astral states of aversion, and desires to release them and gain insight and freedom from bondage to these delusional mental states.

The long-term purpose of meditation practice is to be able to integrate all experience beyond threshold one, which includes all our personal untransformed experiences. Then the second stage is to be able to go beyond threshold two, so as to access transcendent resources that go beyond the limited personal as the self merges into the realms of non-self. This is the place where consciousness soul fuses into spirit-self to become life-spirit or Buddha —the one that is able to flourish in the realms of the spirit, the one who is able to cross the second threshold — because through continuous and regular meditation practices one has created a pathway within one's own body and soul to the transpersonal realm. Crossing the second threshold is the reward for work in meditation practice that diligently transforms the inner unintegrated life. Across the second threshold one meets the Bodhisattva who, out of this transpersonal realm of the spirit, vows to return to the incarnated visible realms as a bearer of light and healing to all who suffer:

All beings I must set free
The whole world of living beings
I must rescue from the terrors of birth, of old age, of sickness, of death and rebirth, of all kinds of moral offence, of all states of woe.
(Conze et al, 1954:pp.131f)

When the astral has been transformed into compassion mind or sentient soul, then wisdom mind or intellectual soul results in an awareness of inter-being. This is the place of consciousness soul which is the natural pathway across the second threshold. Here, one traverses the threshold, not in fear of possession of dark beings, nor in terror of being flooded or overwhelmed by the power of this realm. Here, one has earned the right to cross the second threshold by having diligently transformed the states found across the first threshold; the states of one's own mind with all their shadows, traumas and despair. These have now been transformed into compassion mind so that one acts from a place of equanimity, kindness, compassion and joy in another's joy. We come to live out of what, in Buddhism, is termed as the 'four divine abodes. We will then find that our inner and outer actions and thoughts are warmed by the good heart, the compassionate heart, which is at the centre of a healthy human being. Warming our thoughts, infusing our deeds with compassion, our life has a new quality:

> The transformation that occurs when practice
> becomes an awakening from the self-centred dream
> is a transformation in our emotional life. In the
> deluded mind, fear, anger sadness, disgust, shame
> and distraction predominate. In the awakened mind
> equanimity, love and joy predominate and wisdom
> emerges the ability to make appropriate responses to
> life which are based on seeing life as a whole, not on
> a perception which is narrowed down to self-interest.
> The transformation does not annihilate the negative
> emotions. It shifts them from self-centred motivation
> to a life centre motivation ... (Dawson, 2000:p.13).

Conclusion

Meditation as a pathway to personal growth promises a sustainable well-tested route with a long history of proven success in creating well-being in eastern cultures. Recent research in western culture is also demonstrating its effectiveness in managing and improving a range of mental and physical health conditions. It is a well-trodden pathway whose foundation in life is strong, whose steps are well made and whose track leads to skilful outcomes. It empowers one through dedicated practice on a regular basis to create the inner structures within the human being to cross both the first and second thresholds with sustainability, strength, inner maturity and vision. It is grounded yet expansive, embodied yet transpersonal. It must be a recommended personal-growth pathway for the modern world, for it has the capacity to take us to the core of our human being-ness, to integrate the self and to arrive at an inner place of stillness amid the turbulent times in which we live. We can find the place of clear awakening to the true nature of ourself, where we can understand the reality free from the torrents and turbulent storms of aversion, desire, ignorance, greed and hatred that disturb our mind's vision. Our heart's desire for these states of calmness is well echoed by Rumi:

I want these words to stop.
Calm the chattering mind, my soul.
No more camel's milk.
I want silent water to drink,
And the majesty of a clear waking.
(Rumi, 2007:p.122)

11. Narcissism: roadblock on the pathway

Withhold admiration from a narcissist and be disliked.
Give it and be treated with indifference.
— Mason Cooley

Critiques of the personal-growth pathways lead eventually to the problem of narcissism which is the preoccupation and focus upon one's own well-being, to the exclusion of the well-being of others. It is coupled with the active exploitation and manipulation of others for one's personal need for gratification, adoration and exaltation. Salerno (2005:p.39) argues that the self-help personal-growth movement is a breeding ground for narcissists because it encourages individuals to be self-centred to such a degree that they have difficulty relating to others and considering the common good. They believe they are omnipotent and can do anything they want at the expense of others. He argues that the personal-growth industry is guilty of promoting an 'all you gotta do is want it' approach to life, which is a licence to do what you want, to get what you want (McIllwain, 2006). This is a simplistic view of what produces narcissism for this state of being, without empathetic feeling, is far more pervasively toxic than just trying to get what you want. While it can certainly be found among some leaders and followers within the personal-growth industry, it is endemic to contemporary western society which 'places the achievement of success above the need to love and to be loved'(Lowen, 1984).

Christopher Lash (1979) went further and argued that as an entire culture we have become seduced by narcissism, as we have become a greedy, frivolous, self-centred society:

> The new narcissist is haunted not by guilt but by anxiety. He seeks not to inflict his own certainties on others but to find a meaning in life. Liberated from the superstitions of the past, he doubts even the reality of his own existence. Superficially realized and tolerant, he finds little use for dogmas of racial and ethnic purity but at the same time forfeits the security of group loyalties and regards everyone as a rival for the favours conferred by a paternalistic state ... fiercely competitive in his demand for approval and acclaim, acquisitive in the sense that his cravings have no limit, he lives in a state of restless, perpetually unsatisfied desire. (Lash, 1979)

While Lash tended to focus on social causes of narcissism, psychological work on narcissism has been completed by a number of prominent psychotherapists who see narcissism as a result of particular types of adverse childhood bonding experiences with caregivers. Freud identified it as early as 1914, and described pathological narcissism as a primitive defence mechanism to survive early childhood trauma, particularly in relation to the bond with the primary caregivers where the child retreats away from their unsatisfactory love and back to self-love. In the retreat, the child may feel hostility to the parents for their inadequacy and the child's experience of forced premature self-sufficiency. As an adult, this person 'cannot reconcile intense and overwhelming feelings of dependency with a necessary belief in omnipotent self-sufficiency and the conflict is expressed as a craving for admiration' (Hotchkiss, 2005). Further research has identified a number of factors contributing to its growth. Imbesi (1999) notes that the developing child needs to experience boundaries and limits to his power to curb the growth of narcissism. Barry et al (2007) find that low self-esteem underlies narcissistic behaviours and Horton et al (2006) state that psychological control by parents is also associated with narcissistic behaviour. There is a spectrum of narcissistic behaviours from the mild to the severe. Vaknim (2006) lists the nine features, of which five must be met, that are used to identify someone as having narcissistic personality disorder in The Diagnostic and Statistical Manual of Mental Disorders (DSM_IV), published by the American Psychiatric Association. These are that the individual:

1. Feels grandiose and self-important, which includes exaggerating accomplishments, talents, skills, contacts and personality traits to the point of lying and insisting on being recognised as superior but without the commensurate achievements;

2. Has obsessions with fantasies of unlimited success, fame, or bodily beauty or sexual performance or intellectual brilliance;

3. Believes they are unique and special and should only be associated with high status people;

4. Requires excessive affirmation and attention;

5. Demands automatic and full compliance with their unreasonable expectations;

6. Uses others for their own ends;

7. Is devoid of empathy and unwilling to accept choices of others;

8. Is envious of others and seeks to hurt or destroy such objects;

9. Feels superior, invincible, omnipresent, and rages when confronted or contradicted by people considered inferior.

(http://samvak.tripod.com/npdglance.html)

In What makes Narcissists tick? Krajce notes the eight red flags of narcissistic behaviour are identified in human relationships. These are, the individual who:

1. puts on a conspicuous display of goodness and kindness;

2. damages the images of most others;

3. has a history of past upheavals;

4. is hated for mysterious reasons by people close to them;

5. exhibits unnatural and perplexing behaviours;

6. is a control freak who tramples privacy and boundaries;

7. is extremely self-absorbed;

8. has a hostile reaction to attention and credit given to others.

(http://www.narcissism.operationdoubles.com/ narcissism_red_flags.htm)

According to Vaknin (2003) approximately 0.5–1% of the general population has Narcissistic Personality Disorder

(NPD) and the majority of these are men. However, many more people manifest these clusters of qualities and go undiagnosed.

Narcissistic personalities and behaviours profoundly affect the adult workplace and intimate relationships in an adverse manner. In personal-growth books, like Living with a Narcissist by Richard (2005), writers share experiences of bewilderment, heartbreak and recovery in living through relationships with a narcissistic partner. Narcissists are usually charismatic and self-confident, often concerned with appearance and, initially, they can be very charming. They have a series of often short-lived, exploitative, personal relationships or partners on the side to keep their self-esteem inflated.

Research on the toxic workplace and narcissistic bosses continues to emerge. Chatterjee et al (2007) note that in the computer industry narcissistic bosses favour bold actions that attract attention, resulting in big wins or losses, but the firm's performance is generally no better nor worse than firms with non-narcissistic leaders. And one could add that workplace relationships are a great deal more supportive and healthy when the bosses are not narcissists. Vogel (2006) describes how narcissists are drawn to ego-intensive professions like marketing, entrepreneurship and corporate management because here they have a stage for their public performances that give them the adulation upon which they thrive. The downside of their leadership is temper tantrums, unreasonable expectations, inability to work as a team member, rage at being challenged or questioned, claiming the work of support staff as their own, and denying praise to anyone but themself. When things fail, they are completely willing to blame someone else without remorse or doubt because failure is always the other person's fault.

Narcissistic people with an inflated sense of self-confidence and ego, often coupled with charisma, do become leaders in the personal-growth industry, particularly in either secular or spiritual positions of power, influence and wealth, with a following of people looking for the way, for more skills and for more self-confidence. Such leaders are usually very persuasive, carve out an impressive image in the short-term and only some weeks and months after the participants have signed up do the cracks begin to show, that is, if the participants are not so deeply under their charismatic spell that they notice them. Common cracks include: sexual and financial exploitation of participants; mental and emotional control and manipulation; expecting followers to live by a different set of behaviour standards and rules than they do themselves; saying the right things but doing the opposite; showing superficial, emotional rapport when they gain to benefit from such a display of emotion; using guilt or shame to manipulate people into completing a course, or staying when they want to leave; undermining the reputation and credibility of people who leave or disagree; and a demonstrated lack of integrity and authenticity across a broadening range of issues. They have scant regard for moral codes of any sort, lack self-restraint in response to other people and see themselves free to create their own lifestyles. Samford (2004:p.41) also notes a frequent absence of qualifications and training to deliver the personal-growth packages they claim to be able to deliver. This places the participants at risk in the hands of people who rely on their charisma rather than their skills to complete psychological processes that can leave participants vulnerable and exposed, without adequate support and follow-up because the charismatic leader does not know what they don't know.

The case study below illustrates the hazards and complexities of narcissism in the personal growth industry.

Case study

Adam was forty-two years of age, and looked in very good shape. He attended the gym daily and his body looked fit, while he had captivating blue eyes, dark hair and an irresistible smile. I suspected that he dressed impeccably in Italian suits and shoes. He had a charming presence on first meeting, was a magnet for beautiful and intelligent women and had never married because, in his own words, 'so many women, so little time.' Adam ran a private business in the personal-growth industry where he trained healers with a new type of healing which, he told me, created the light workers needed to heal the planet. He claimed that he was a channel for this remarkable unique knowledge to humanity. It was his special calling and his remarkable gift which he had come to teach others how to do.

Adam had a remarkable capacity to talk as though he knew the answers to the profound questions of meaning in the modern world, and he spoke with conviction about the pathway to the healing he offered, which was the best thing on the market. There was no question that he had charisma and could sell himself and his product with an ease and confidence that was impressive. However, in the entire rendition of his life story, I did not sense any feelings of joy, grief, love or loss. There was simply a sustained dramatic performance that, while engaging, was deeply unsatisfying if one was seeking to follow his feelings. It was as if his body, for all its fine-chiselled musculature from hours at the gym, was made of marble instead of human flesh.

He boasted endlessly about his personal-growth training business that had run very successfully for over a decade. He drove the latest model BMW and owned several townhouses as well as a waterside home. Adam assured me that he was born with this special healing talent and that he had worked out how to train others to manifest their healing talents. Usually, his courses were full, with waiting lists and for some reason were almost always full of affluent, bored or depressed women in their thirties and forties, who found Adam inspirational. He did not find it difficult to extend his courses from one year, to two or three years or more, because many of his followers were prepared to spend years of their lives learning from him. In fact, Adam was the textbook charismatic personal-growth guru. He had unique talent, wealth, influence and business success. He confided that he had had a series of relationships with women who he always misjudged as attractive, healthy, intelligent and companionable, and who destroyed the quality of the relationship with their emotional instability or physical ill health. He was pleased that he had no children and spent large amounts of time playing golf and scuba diving.

Adam had a glitch in his armour against the world. He knew the healing he did was very special, stunning in its results, but his lack of credentials enraged him when his work was dismissed or not recognised by other high status professionals. He strove desperately for validation beyond his own knowledge of his talent. Wealth and adoring women were simply not enough of a conquest for Adam. He wanted recognition in the healing industry that he was the best.

Adam had joined a training diploma course in health science, not because he believed they could teach him anything but because he wanted the qualification. Ironically, this was the cause of his angst and his appearance as a client in counselling. He had failed one of the course units and had been asked to repeat it the following year, and he was furious because he knew he could do it and do it well and he was enraged by the indignity of it all. The teachers had failed him and he was enraged. His current partner had suggested that he come to discuss his feelings about the injustice of it all with a counsellor.

Adam was demonstrating the defences of his narcissism and insisted throughout the session that there was no part of the problem that he was responsible for. It was his teachers' unjust assessment practices; if only they could have recognised his talent they would never have treated him like that. In fact, Adam ruminated on taking legal action against them for delaying his graduation from the course. He had all the behaviours that traditionally make it so hard to work with the narcissist, even if they do come to therapy, which is rare. They tend to defend themselves against taking any responsibility for their problem, and project their problem onto others, who they either despise as inferiors or feel aggressive towards because of their superior power, status or wealth.

I cannot say that I succeeded in helping Adam to overcome his angst towards those who had failed him, despite my best efforts. I did to get him to find where in his body he felt the anger and to step into his body and experience the trauma that was underlying it, using an anger sequence (Sherwood, 2004), and he did find himself as a young boy ignored by his cold and distant father. He did not like what he found and he did not like being vulnerable and exposed, even when he was shown skills to resource and nurture that lost part of himself and to retain his strength and dignity. He came back for a second session but was well defended this time and refused to step into his body. He simply play-acted, turned on his defensive charm, and refused to go anywhere near his bodily stored feelings. He deliberately blocked any intervention to access what he was really feeling in his body. I could not say the therapy was really effective for him as a person but, at least after discussion, he decided legal action simply was not worth the effort and he would go elsewhere to obtain qualifications, with people who could really appreciate his talent.

Summary of the outcomes of healthy and unhealthy personal growth

The narcissist, however successful in worldly acquisition and, whatever their personal-growth claims, is unable to demonstrate the outcomes of healthy personal growth.

1. I am more present in my daily life

As Lowen (1995) notes compassionately: 'there is something crazy about a person who is out of touch with the reality of his or her being-the body and its feelings.' The narcissist flourishes in appearance by repressing the reality of bodily experiences wherein is contained all their emotional traumas of abandonment, rejection and/or abuse that has characterized their childhoods, and against which their bodies are armoured. As Vogel (2006) notes, their self-confidence and stated self-regard belies an intense need for approval, that often leads them to rages and defensiveness if they feel unappreciated, challenged or criticized. They do anything to avoid being present to what is really going on at an emotional level. Like Adam, who would focus on anyone he thought was responsible for his failure in his course, rather than on himself and his own blinding arrogance to his abilities.

2. I am empowered to shape my destiny

The narcissist fells empowered to shape their life destiny and usually takes control of shaping the life destinies of others because of their belief in their own superiority. Adam was convinced that he was the answer to his followers' need for guidance and direction in their lives. However, since narcissists project their frustration onto others, it is never their fault; they are unable to be truly awake to what their relationship dynamic is with the world, so live upon the surface of life in a superficial connection with the world, and out of real touch with whom they are and their destiny.

3. I am increasingly free from reactions

Full-blown narcissists live lives of constant drama and fight with those who challenge their dominance and competence, and manipulate others through mock feelings of fear, anger, rage, grief and loss, colouring others as black while they stand on the high moral ground. Their lives are often a roller coaster of drama, their pathways strewn with feuds with others who do not recognise their competence, specialness or talent. They live in a whirlpool of reactions. In contrast, moderate narcissists who drive through life hogging the road, siphoning off extra resources and feeding off others are shown, in research, to report that they are less likely to be depressed, sad or anxious, and report les stress and less vulnerability to loss and grief (Vogel, 2006). They may have few reactions, although others around them have many, as neither insight or compassion are part of their world experience. Adam was this type of person. His relationships were useful to give him what he needed and he was very keen to foreclose on the one trauma in his life by rationalizing it as the teacher's incompetence and moving on to where he could be recognised and respected for the genius he believed himself to be.

4. I am more fully who I am: 'self-actualization' and 'self-transcendence'

The tragedy for the narcissistic person is that their relationships are empty, limited, cut off from their feelings. Their life is run by visions, goals, targets, performances and they stand ultimately alone, isolated from loved ones. They are cut off from the love of others, but also of love of self. As Lowen notes so accurately:

> narcissism denotes an investment in one's image as opposed to one's self. Narcissists love their image, not their real self. They have a poor sense of self: They are not self-directed. Instead their activities are directed toward the enhancement of their image, often at the expense of the self. (Lowen, 1997:p.25)

Their life is not characterized by the widening of genuine human connections based on empathy and sensitivity to others, but rather they are isolated socially in the degree to which their behaviour towards others is ruthless, exploitative, sadistic, destructive, dismissive or hostile.

Narcissism and the holistic model of personal growth for body, soul and spirit

Narcissism is an arrested state of personal growth. So, in light of the holistic model of personal growth, what is avoided, blocked and distorted? To understand this we need to distinguish between two main types of narcissistic characters: the one who focuses entirely on his special bodily sexual prowess, (the 'phallic narcissistic character'), and the one who focuses upon his unique, outstanding intellectual, spiritual or personal power. The former think, as they walk down the street, that all women are waiting to fall into their arms, while the latter believe that specially appointed assistants should make way for them as they walk down the street because of their superior stature and glory (Lowen, 1997:p.18). Some people manage to incorporate both types of narcissism into their characters. Both types of narcissism can have the quality of charisma which attracts others to engage in the dynamic by bestowing upon them attention, praise, respect, obedience and, at times, adoration.

To understand where narcissists flourish let us return to the holistic model of body, soul and spirit. Both the phallic narcissistic character and the narcissistic character at all costs, avoid the true feeling life, the place of sentient soul wherein is developed empathy and compassion. The phallic narcissistic character remains anchored in body and in this over-incarnated position refuses to enter into sentient soul at any time. Their feelings are driven by body: physical, etheric and sentient body which drives the basic animal gratification needs. For the phallic narcissistic, relationships with others are characterized by sexual exploitation, manipulation and cruelty without remorse. They are relatively easy to identify because they leave a trail of ex-lovers who are mad, sick or, in some other way, deranged, desperate and neurotic, while they move without trauma from one beautiful and adoring lover to the next, quite unperturbed by the trail of broken hearts and minds they leave in their wake.

The second type of narcissist avoids their soul or feeling life imprinted in sentient soul at any cost, but they raft themselves above in intellectual soul. These people are under-incarnated and avoid contact with their feeling life through a range of defence mechanisms, the most common of which are intellectualizing and rationalizing.

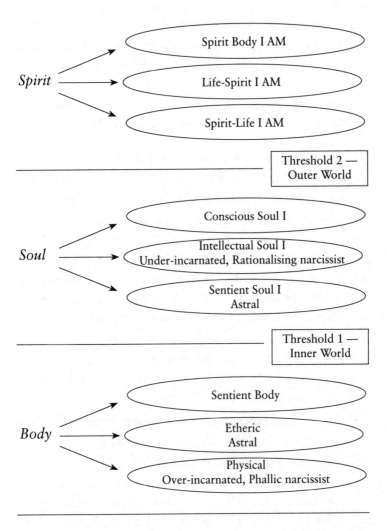

While many people use the defence mechanisms of intellectualizing and rationalizing and are not narcissists, these defence mechanisms are the specialities of these types of narcissists. We need to examine them in some detail to be aware of the pervasive, blinding power of narcissists who use these defence mechanisms. They are used abundantly by narcissistic teachers and gurus in the personal-growth movement. The following six characteristics are demonstrated by charismatic narcissistic teachers and are anchored in intellectual soul, using the defence mechanisms of intellectualizing and rationalizing to create a potent brew for exploitation of the followers:

1. They have completed all their personal-growth work and have arrived at whatever state of enlightenment they are claiming to teach as the goal of their process

2. They demonstrate impressive knowledge and information about their subject but it is as dry as dead men's bones as there is no anchoring of this knowledge in the heart's compassion. The knowledge is often profoundly vast on the subject but it lacks the warmth of knowledge infused by the heart's feelings and transmuted into living wisdom.

3. They know it all and dismiss or belittle any challenges to their worldview or the information they are providing.

4. They respond to genuine feelings demonstrated by anyone with a feeling-less intellectual solution.

5. They justify and rationalize all their behaviours even when they are avowedly outrageous or against the rules for the followers. One example is that paedophilia is alright for me because I am blessing

the child with special spiritual power through having sex with them.

6. They shift realities with clever intellectual arguments and rationalizations so that the followers are often confused and uncertain so accept the changes even though, in their feelings, they may have some misgivings. George Orwell's Animal Farm illustrates so well how the charismatic narcissistic pigs reshape reality on a regular basis to support their ever-increasing power and control over the animals. Subtlety, but cleverly they move reality from: 'All animals are equal' to 'All animals are equal but some are more equal than others' to justify their right to exploit the other animals even until death.

7. They shift blame for anything that goes wrong, on the follower's lack of progress on the personal-growth pathway, to anyone convenient, other than themselves. They always rationalize why they are not responsible for anything that goes wrong. It is always somebody else's fault.

Safely rafted above sentient soul where their true feelings and experiences are stored, they have effectively had an emotional bypass. The tragedy is that they can never reach the state of consciousness soul of true human awakening. Herein alone, is the experience of deep connectedness with self, the other and the world. They are in denial of their true self and distant from the knowledge of their own feelings. They are cut off in the fantasy world created and sustained through their own intellectualizing. In the windows of opportunity where there is a potential ray of light into their feeling life, they usually close the shutters and seek further intellectual explanations for their woundedness, rather than actually going to the feelings in the wound and beholding the pain and healing it. They remain in the world of deluded intellectualism which can only lead to death, not liberation as the Buddha so insightfully captures:

> If a man has been wounded by an arrow thickly
> smeared with poison, and his friends ... were to
> procure for him a physician and the sick man were to
> say: 'I will not have the arrow taken out until I have
> learnt whether the man who wounded me belonged
> to the warrior caste, or the Brahmin caste, or the
> agricultural caste'... this man would die. (Pali Canon)

What then of the followers who provide the other side of the Velcro of the narcissistic relationship? The narcissist may provide the hooks, but the followers provide the loops to attach to the hooks. There are two main types of people who embrace the narcissist because the followers are available to be exploited because they have needs which 'fit' with what the narcissist offers. The first type are those in touch with their trauma in their sentient soul, driven by their aversions and desires and confusion, uncertain of direction in their life, unable to find their way to a meaningful happy life. They feel overwhelmed by their own fears, uncertainties and sense of self-fragmentation. In brief, caught up in the whirlpool of the astral life without adequate tools to navigate their way, they are vulnerable. They are readily available links to the narcissist who is most often charismatic, can offer a vision, a purpose, appears very self-confident and offers a way through the morass of confusion, inadequacy and purposelessness. The less society provides meaningful, practical, supportive skills and processes to deal with emotional trauma and unresolved aversion and desires, the more people are seduced by the charismatic leader, for such leaders can fill some of the gaps left by the failure of the traditional institutions to nurture people's hearts and support people in emotional crisis.

Currently, the gap is left primarily to the advertising industry with its glib message that one can buy heart and soul and happiness of all kinds by consuming more and more; a message whose misleading promises are increasingly transparent. The whirlpools of sentient soul can be frightening, overwhelming and depleting for the individual, left alone to struggle in the turbulent waters. When the charismatic narcissist throws a life raft it can look good, better than drowning. These people need to acquire intensive skills to manage this life offered by good quality counselling, meditation practices and the like. Our culture needs to go further and begin emotional literacy schooling as an equal partner to cognitive literacy. Then, as adults, people will have the tools to continue to handle the maelstroms thrown up by sentient soul without having to resort to numbing themselves through prescription drugs, or by becoming prey to charismatic narcissists in personal or group relationships.

The second type of follower, who often becomes a close confidant of the charismatic narcissistic leader or teacher avoids the sentient soul of the turbulent astral life at all costs and lives in intellectual soul. They use the defence mechanisms of intellectualizing and rationalizing to create a meaningful niche for themselves, rationalize their life purpose and avoid feelings at any cost, preferring to explain away their experiences as a much safer option. Such people are emotionally needy but have kept their sense of self and purpose together through the mental activities in their lives. They are seduced intellectually by the charismatic narcissist because he promises them answers to their questions, has confidence and conviction of his rightness, and competency that is impressive. Out of touch with their own feeling life, they miss the subtle nuances of the narcissistic out-of-touchness with feelings. They fail to see the dryness in his knowledge, the lack of empathy and feeling in his teaching, the lack of humility and awareness of his limitations. Usually, the first wake-up signs for these followers, is when the narcissistic leader becomes involved in exploitative behaviours, either sexually, financially or otherwise, that are outside of the agreed rules. In this situation, they are faced with confronting the narcissistic leader and risking his rage, denial and their exclusion from the group, or simply living quietly with it, believing the leader's justificatory speeches and rationales for their excessive behaviours. If they perceive the deep moral ravines in the narcissistic leader's behaviours and leave, they forfeit their investment in the vision, purpose and future of the narcissistic leader's world to which they have heavily subscribed. Their healing is to reclaim their own heart, to complete the work of their sentient soul so they may build their knowledge on the firm foundation of their own heart. Then, and only then, can intellectual soul be transformed into wisdom mind. It then becomes a fitting complement for compassion mind, which is the fruit of the work of healing the traumas, the aversion and desires that trouble the sentient soul. Only then is intellectual soul not vulnerable to the persuasive charismatic narcissist, because one will sense immediately the lack of true feeling, humility, sensitivity to human suffering and connectedness and compassion for humanity and the world.

Conclusion

What would be the basic qualities of the reliable and safe teacher who can genuinely facilitate personal growth? Such a person stands in counterpoint to the proud, charismatic, narcissistic leader and teacher who has evaded the truth of their own feeling life, their own aversions and desires and imprisoned themself in a lonely tower of grandiose superiority. The genuine teacher is truly supportive of sustainable personal growth and is best described in a conversation between Arjuna and Lord Krishna in the ancient Hindu text, The Bhagavad Gita.

> Arjuna: What O Krishna is the description of him who has steady wisdom and is merged in the superconscious state? How does he speak, how does he sit, how does the walk?
> Lord Krishna: He who is unattached every where who is neither delighted at receiving good, or dejected by evil, is poised in wisdom.
> Arjuna: How will a person poised in wisdom look at things?
> Lord Krishna: men of self-knowledge look with equal vision on a Brahman (highest spiritual caste) and imbued with learning and humility a cow, an elephant, a dog and an outcast.
> (http://www.bhagavad.gita.org/index-english.html)

12. Personal growth: beyond the destination

I know what should be known
What should be cultivated, I have cultivated
What should be abandoned that I have abandoned
Hence, I am the Buddha, the Awakened One.
— The Buddha

At the heart of personal growth is the notion of 'the self'. Self is to be developed, improved, to become more skilful, more competent and more integrated as a functioning whole. We speak of self-growth, self-esteem, self-worth, and 'self-actualization', which Maslow described initially as the culmination of the human growth journey, and which today we call 'personal growth'. Such a self-actualized person has transcended the problems of becoming who they wish to be and can:

function in growth promoting ways in their world, so that there is a good correlation between subjective delight in the experience, impulse for the experience or wish for it and basic need for the experience. Only such people uniformly yearn for what is good for them and for others and then are able wholeheartedly to enjoy it and approve of it. (Maslow, 1959:p.129).

However, Maslow (1968) became concerned that what he observed was that some people pursuing personal growth and fully actualizing themselves, failed to become more connected to other people, failed to become willing to invest energy in the well-being of the whole. They seemed stuck at an egocentric position where the resources and activities in the world were directed narrowly at themselves and their own perceived benefit: this is the 'I, myself and me' syndrome, which leads to greed, injustice, cruelty and, by default, narcissism, because of the absence of concern with the consequences of one's actions for other people in this global village. Maslow (1973) suggested the need for a further stage of human growth, which he described as 'self-transcendence.' This laid the foundations for the growth of the concept of the transpersonal which sees interconnectedness with each other, and with the world, as essential to optimize human psychological health. This became the basis for transpersonal psychology which was profoundly influenced by eastern psychology as expounded by Ken Wilber (1983). At the heart of this psychology is transcendence of self as a limited bounded entity. Instead, we conceive the highest forms of human growth as the dissolution of the boundaries of self into an awareness of what Thich Nhat Hahn terms 'inter-being', the place described as 'not-self or 'non-self' in Buddhist psychology. This is the place beyond clutching onto personal growth; the place that ensures that we do not become trapped in the dead-end road of self-pre-occupation and self-adoration which ultimately leads us to a sense of meaninglessness, limitedness and, in some cases, narcissistic stasis. We live, but we do not flourish. We are highly competent, but we do not realize the joy of being. This joy and serenity comes from awakening to boundlessness, and to limitless oneness. This is the experience of complete fulfilment. It has been written about by many. The British poet Tennyson described it as:

> All at once, as it were out of the intensity of consciousness of individuality, the individuality itself seemed to dissolve and fade away into boundless being and this is not a confused state but the clearest of the clearest, the surest of the surest ... utterly beyond words. (cited in Alexander et al, 1990:p.313).

The movement from self to non-self

Welwood (1983) in his seminal work, Awakening the Heart, refers to the different conceptions of human growth in western and eastern psychologies. How does personal growth of western psychology fit with the journey of discovering a larger awareness and interconnectedness with a transcendent reality that is the goal of eastern psychology? What relevance have the notions of self to Buddhist psychology, which is so focused on the notion of interconnectedness, or what Thigh Nat Hahn (1985) describes as 'inter-being', referred to in different Buddhist traditions as 'not-self ' or 'non self'? As Engler noted, Buddhism sees this self-focus as a 'state of arrested growth. (1986:p.47).

Western psychology, despite its diverse schools, has been concerned almost wholly with the growth of the self. Burns (1971) effectively reviews the variations on working with self-growth in western psychology noting that it has amassed a variety of tools for dealing with the notion of self which it treats as a discrete subject. The strength of this focus on the need to develop a healthy self, is the cultivation of a responsible, integrated self, with precise tools for dealing with the day-to-day issues of self-experience, including relationships, intimacy and vocation. However, Rubin, (1996:p.68) notes the problems of a fixed, personally developed self, which denies the continuously growing quality of human consciousness and the non-self experiences of interconnectedness. The limits of this self-focus lead to a self-isolation and self-consuming interest. Neither pathway produces optimum psychological health, and often leads to problems of narcissism, depression, addiction and anxiety. Buddhist psychology provides the way through the no through road of self-preoccupation. Buddhism focuses on flowing mental states, impermanency and a non-discrete sense of experience summarized in the concept of not-self or inter-being. It facilitates the ability to access meaning and experiences which connect with the numinous. It enables one to focus on the present moment, without attachment to particular mental states or the limitations of the 'self' concept. The concept of non-self expands the arena of mental health action for western psychology, giving a concrete vision of the need for connectedness in a meaningful way with others and with the natural world, in order to have robust psychological health (Rubin, 1996).

This does not dismiss the need to focus on the self as the core of human growth. All individuals need first to deal with the trauma and abuse that fragments their sense of an integrated healthy self. A solid integrated concept of self is the foundation of the step towards the experience of interconnectedness and inter- being. The study of self is a crucial step that cannot be bypassed on the way to an enlightened state of non-self or inter-being. As the famous Zen master, Dogen, so accurately summarized:

To study the self is to forget the self.
To forget the self is to be one with others.
(Epstein, 1996:p.20)

In order to have a non-self, one must first have a self, and we benefit from some of the techniques and skills for developing a healthy integrated self, while remaining unattached to the concept of self as a permanent construct; the ultimate destination of human growth. It becomes a critical stop on the unending journey towards the experience of non-self, inter-being and interconnectedness. Rubin (1996:p.77) sees the benefits of both a self-focus and a non-self perspective on human life and experience. The self-focus gives us the capacity to shape goals and identify the patterns of the self, while the non-self-consciousness opens us to our human capacity to experience art, love, music and dance in their boundary-dissolving moments of union, flowing with the pervasive consciousness of all beings.

If we become overly attached to the notion of self, we can fall short of moving through to the transcendent experiences which give our lives such richness and expansiveness beyond the limits of our self-serving consciousness. Rather than cling to fixed notions such a personal growth as the point of our arrival, we gain by moving to the notion of consciousness as continual flow and change, recognising that all things are impermanent and there is only the present moment to fully enjoy. Epstein captures the movement:

The shift [is] from an appetite based, spatially
conceived self preoccupied with a sense of what is
lacking to a breath based, and temporally conceived
self capable of spontaneity and aliveness ...
(Epstein, 1995:p.147)

From emotional attachment to emotional non-attachment

While preoccupied with the notion self we cling to every feeling allowing it to define who we are, who we like and dislike, and to drive our life choices. When the feelings are negative, such as fear, anger or hatred, we find that the quality of our life declines rapidly and we begin to feel trapped in a dark place. We often find ourselves driven to express these emotions of self or to repress them, but there is an alternative method of not clinging to them but rather observing them as part of a continuous flow of consciousness and experience (Epstein, 1995:p.101). Freeing oneself from attachment to one's aversions and desires, and observing them as impermanent states of disequilibrium, rather than being driven by them, is an essential goal. The focus on non-attachment, meditation and breathing techniques to calm the emotions, leads to an expansive sense of self which is eventually capable of the dissolution of self boundaries and the expansion into the flow of consciousness. The French playwright, Ionesco (1971), describes this peak experience as immense serene joy:

> Once long ago, I was sometimes overcome by a sort of grace, a euphoria. It was as if first of all, every motion, every reality was emptied of its content. After this, it was as if I found myself suddenly at the centre of pure ineffable existence. I became one with the one essential reality, when along with an immense serene joy, I was overcome ... (cited in Alexander et al, 1990:p. 313).

The holistic model: beyond personal growth

If we are to understand more deeply the movement from
the personal integrated self in personal growth to the
limitless boundaries of the not-self, we must look again at
the ninefold model which represents the incarnation process
from the limitless realms into the realms of individuated
consciousness; from spirit into body. In reverse, this model
can also indicate the way back to the fusion with the realms
of consciousness beyond delineated forms. In essence, this
model is about spiritualizing the body so that eventually
the body itself fuses with eternal realms of consciousness
without boundaries of a separate skin-encapsulated self.
This can be elucidated by focusing on consciousness soul,
for this is where the true nature of the 'I', that part of the
individuated eternal consciousness, manifests itself, free from
the aversion and desires of the astral feeling life. Here, one
finds the space of equanimity which is beyond clinging to
feelings of fear, anger, hatred that govern the astral states
of consciousness, called 'ordinary mind' in Buddhism. It
is here, in consciousness soul, that we gain insight to our
true nature, for here we are capable of insight. This is a
consequence of work done on the astral body, particularly
sentient soul, to free oneself from the imprints of aversion
and desire, sympathy and antipathy, which transform it into
compassion mind. Then, the knowledge understood and
accumulated in intellectual soul is transformed into wisdom
mind, and together wisdom and compassion create the depth
of insight that enables us to begin to dwell in consciousness
soul. It is here that we recognise the interconnectedness of
all beings. It is here, that freed from aversion and desire, and
the pushes and pulls of the astral life, that we can become

a blessing to the world around us. People like the Dalai Lama, Ghandhi, Nelson Mandala, Aung San Suu Kyi, are inspirational examples of human beings who can act out of consciousness soul. Without any aversion or hatred towards people that others would call enemies, these human beings provide inspirational examples of the place that opens up beyond self-growth. This is the place where one can act out of a flow of common consciousness, the flow of inter-being, and generate goodness for those who lives are touched. Here, one is waking up to the noble nature of human consciousness, known as the spirit, which is otherwise the hidden element in everything manifest.

The stronger the presence of the 'I' in consciousness, the more it becomes master of the astral or sensory soul life. A wonderful example of this process of staying with consciousness soul rather than reverting to the astral life, was demonstrated during a media interview with a great Buddhist lama who spoke with great clarity, dignity, humour and equanimity. He had been unjustly imprisoned in Tibet by the Chinese government for twenty years, during which he had suffered and witnessed the most appalling forms of torture and cruelty. As a consequence, his physical health was very fragile, but clearly his mental health was robust. When asked by the interviewer whether he had ever felt defeated while in the prison he replied: 'I was nearly defeated once. On that day, I nearly lost my compassion for the guard who was torturing the prisoners. But I breathed deeply and did not go to hatred.'

When the spirit or the 'I AM' so penetrates the astral body that it is vibrationally transformed into higher consciousness it becomes what, in this model, is called 'spirit self'. If we not only think differently but feel differently, then the I AM has penetrated the etheric body and this can be raised vibrationally at that moment to the second element of spirit the life-spirit. In eastern traditions, this is know as the buddhi, the place of awakening. Here, we know clearly what is to be cultivated and what is to be abandoned, when to act and when to refrain from acting. It is the place of profound equanimity where we see the flow of consciousness. We are the observer beyond the boundaries of the self, part of the flow of the eternal spirit or consciousness. We are the warriors of Shambhala who have conquered aversion and desire within ourselves. Our weapons to maintain the awakened state, and not be overtaken by the delusions of the astral or sensory life, are wisdom and compassion. At this place, we are awake to the knowing that the line between good and evil is within each mind and heart, and the war which must be fought, is within. We remain awake to wisdom and compassion and there arises in that place 'a clear forest pool' within us. Ajahn Chah describes the nature of this inner pool:

All kinds of wonderful, rare creatures will come to drink at the pool, and you will see clearly the nature of all things. You will see many strange and wonderful things come and go, but you will be still. This is happiness of the Buddha (the one who is awake). (Chah, 1994: Preface)

It is the space wherein arises freedom and clarity that are beyond either hope or despair. It is the place that transcends antipathies and sympathies. Here alone, one comes to know an inner peace, and it 'is realizable when individuality melts away and our finiteness no longer oppresses us' (Suzuki, 1970:p.78). We have crossed the second threshold and are capable of states of great bliss and equanimity, where we can flow through the eternal realms not blinded by the glory, power, or ineffable splendour of such heights of consciousness. We can endure the vision, metaphorically, of Moses in the burning bush, of the transfigured Christ arrayed like the sun upon the mountain top, the rainbow emanations of the great Chenrezig upon Mount Kailash, and the transmuting fires breathed by Durga in her cycles of destruction and re-creation.

Here, we will have earned the right to enter the realms of formless consciousness but we will remember the Buddha at this moment arriving at the state of Mahaprajna (great wisdom), who looked back upon the earth and was moved to Mahakaruna (great compassion).

> The enlightened One because He saw Mankind
> drowning in the Great Sea of Birth, Death and
> Sorrows and longed to save them
> For this he was moved to pity (compassion) ...
> Because he saw them consumed by the fires of pain
> and sorrow, yet knowing not where to seek the still
> waters of Samadhi
> For this he was moved to pity ...
> Because He saw men of the world ploughing their
> fields, sowing their seed trafficking, huckstering,
> buying and selling and at the end winning nothing but
> bitterness,
> For this he was moved to pity. (Burt, 1982: p.240)

At this moment, the Buddha resolved to return to the earth in selfless service go facilitate teaching all beings how to become free form suffering. This is the state of the Bodhisattva and the great safeguard against the misuse of power in such high estate. The truly awakened being will choose the Bodhisattva pathway.

SEARCH FOR YOUR SELF

At this moment, may we also look back upon our beloved earth, this planet upon which there is so much unnecessary suffering and likewise be moved from the depths of compassion to return and participate in her healing. We will become realized Bodhisattvas and manifest the great Bodhisattva vows of compassion.

May I be the doctor and the medicine,
And may I be the nurse
For all sick beings in the world
Until everyone is healed.

May a rain of food and drink descend
To clear away the pain of thirst and hunger,
And during eons of famine
May I myself change into food and drink.

May I become an inexhaustible treasure
For those who are poor and destitute,
May I turn into all things they could need
And may these be placed close beside them ...

May I be a protector for those without
A guide for all travellers on the way
May I be a bridge, a boat and a ship
For all who wish to cross the water ...

Just like space
And the great elements such as earth,
May I always support the life
Of all boundless creatures.

And until they pass away from pain
May I also be the source of life
For all the realms of varied beings
That reaches unto the ends of space.
(Shantideva, 2000:pp.33f)

In this gesture of the Bodhisattva we will act from out of
the realms eternal consciousness, part of the flow of formless
consciousness from the place of not-self.

Here a Bodhisattva gives a gift and he does not
apprehend a self, nor a recipient nor a gift: also no
reward of his giving. He surrenders that gift to all
being, but he apprehends neither beings nor self. He
dedicates that gift to supreme enlightenment but he
does not apprehend any enlightenment.
(cited in Conze, 1990:p.137)

Our final step in this transformative pathway in the
boundless realms of consciousness or spirit is when the I
AM works so deeply on the physical body that it too is
transformed vibrationally into the realms of the pure spirit
body. This place is also described as the place of cosmic
consciousness. The highest form of inner work of the I AM
is required to transform the physical body into the Spirit
Body. It is here that all that it means to be fully human, body,
soul and spirit has been integrated into the stream of eternal
consciousness. In this place all that is merges into the formless
and it is the place where, in the words of Chodron (2002),
'To know the self is to forget the self.' It is the realm where
individuated consciousness ceases.

All is one, yet all is formless as captured in the Prajna
Paramita, or Great Heart sutra:

O Sariputra, form does not differ from voidness, and
voidness does not differ from form. Form is voidness
and the void is form: the same is true for feeling,
conception volition and consciousness.
Sariputra, the characteristics of the voidness of all
dhammas are non-arising, non-ceasing, non-defiled,
non-pure, non-increasing, non-decreasing.
Therefore, in the void there is no form, feeling,
conception, volition or consciousness.
No eye, ear, nose, tongue, body or mind, no form,
sound, smell , taste, touch, mind-object, or eye realm
until we come to no realm of consciousness
(www.buddhanet.net)

Here, we are beyond the realms of personal growth,
into the realms of cosmic consciousness, but we need to
remember that these heights can only be reached step-by-
step, by working with the aversion and desires of our astral
bodies on a moment-by-moment basis. The physical, sensory
world must be deeply entered into and aversion and desire
transformed into equanimity. All knowledge, however vast,
cannot become wisdom unless laid upon the foundations of
compassion. We can only know compassion to the degree
that fear, greed, hatred, anger are no longer our blind
companions upon the personal-growth pathway. We need to
get to know them intimately, name them for the limitations
they bring upon our lives and free ourselves from their
bondage. When the foundation is compassion, the personal-
growth pathway must be right. When our own consciousness,
our own autonomous 'I' is strengthened by the processes, so
that it is at the centre of our awakening, then the pathway
must be desirable. Learn tools, acquire skills, learn processes

to assist upon the way, but remember that you must be at the heart of your own journey, for it is your 'I', your highest consciousness, that carries the light that will provide the surest guide. As the Buddha was dying, Ananda, his closest disciple asked him how they should continue their inner awakening to themselves, literally their personal growth, and the Buddha replied with as much relevance then as today:

> Be lamps unto yourselves.
> Be refuges unto yourselves.
> Take yourself no external refuge
> Hold fast to the truth as a lamp.
> Hold fast to the truth as a refuge.
> Look not for a refuge in anyone beside yourselves.
> And those Ananda whether now or after I am dead
> Shall be a lamp unto themselves
> Shall betake themselves as no external refuge
> But holding fast to the truth as their refuge
> Shall not look for refuge to anyone else besides themselves
> It is they who shall reach to the very topmost height;
> But they must be anxious to learn.
> (cited in Conze et al, 1954)

References

Chapter 1

Borysenko, J. and Borysenko, M. (1994) *The Power of the Mind to Heal*. Hay House, CA.

Byrne, R. (2006) *The Secret*. Simon Schuster, New York.

Capra, F. (1975) *The Tao of Physics*. Shambhala, Berkeley.

Conze, E. Horner, I., Snellgrove, D. and Waley, A. (eds.). (1954) *Buddhist Texts through the Ages*. Shambhala, Massachusetts.

De Charms, R. (1968) *Personal Causation: The internal affective Determinants of Behavior*. Academic Press, NY.

Deci, E. and Ryan, R. (1991) 'A motivational Approach to Self: Integration in Personality'. Dienstbier, R. (ed.) Nebraska *Symposium on Motivation: Perspectives on Motivation*, Lincoln, University of Nebraska Press, Vol 38, 237–88.

Deci, E. and Ryan, R. (1985) *Intrinsic Motivation and Self-determination in Human Behaviour*. Plenum, NY.

Evans, M. and Rodger, I. (1992) *Complete Healing: Regaining your Health through Anthroposophical Medicine*. Anthroposophical Press, NY.

Jung, C. (1960) *On the Nature of the Psyche*. Princeton University Press, Princeton.

Lent, R. (2004) 'Towards a unifying theoretical and practical perspective on well-being and psychosocial adjustment'. *Journal of Counselling Psychology*, Vol 51 (4), 482.

Leonhardt, D. (2008) What is self-actualization, anyway? www. thehappyguy.com Accessed 6th January, 2008.

Lindfors, P. (2002) 'Positive health in a group of Swedish white collar workers'. *Psychological Reports*. Vol 91, 839–45.

Lowen, A. (1976) *Bioenergetics*. Penguin, London.

Maslow, A. (1968) *Towards a Psychology of Being*. Nostrad, NY.

Maslow, A. (1959) *New Knowledge in Human Values*. Gateway, Indiana.

McCraty, R., Atkinson, M., Trevor Bradley, R. (2004) 'Electrophysiological Evidence of Intuition: Part 1. The Surprising Role of the Heart.' *The Journal of Alternative and Complementary Medicine*, 10 (1): 133–43.

McCraty, R. and Childe, D. (2003) *The Appreciative Heart: The Psychophysiology of Positive Emotions and Optimal Functioning*. Boulder Creek, CA: The Heart Math Institute. Ebook, www.heartmath.com

McDermott, R. (1994b) *The Essential Steiner*. Rudolf Steiner Press, NY.

McIlwain, D. (2006) 'The charisma of fallible leaders and the limits of self-help.' *Australian Review of Public Affairs*, www.australianreview.net Accessed: 1st May 2006.

Metz, W. (1982) *The Enlightened One. Buddhism*. The World's Religions, Lion, Herts.

Perls, F. (1973) *The Gestalt approach and Eye Witness to Therapy*. Bantam, NY.

Pert, C. (1997) 'Neuropeptides are chemoattractants for human monocytes and tumour cells: A basis for mind-body communication', *Gawler, Science, Passion and Healing*, Gawler Foundation, Victoria.

Reich, W. (1951) *Selected Writings: An introduction to Orgonomy*. Farrar, Straus and Giroux, NY.

Rogers, C. (1961) *On becoming a Person*. Houghton Mifflin, Boston.

Ryan, R. and Frederick, C. (1997) 'On energy, personality and health: Subjective vitality as a dynamic reflection of well-being.' *Journal of Personality*, Vol 65 (3), 529–65.

Ryan, R., Deci, E. and Grolnick, W. (1995) 'Autonomy, relatedness and the self: Their relation to growth and psychopathology.' In: *Cicchetti and Cohen (eds.) Growthal Psychopathology: Theory and Methods*, Vol 1, 618–55, Riley, NY.

Ryff, C. and Singer, B. (1998a) 'The contours of positive human health'. *Psychological Inquiry*, Vol 9 (1), 1–28.

Ryff, C. and Singer, B. (1998b) 'Human health: New directions for the next millennium.' *Psychological Inquiry*, Vol 9 (1), 69–85.

Ryff, C. (1995) 'Psychological well-being in adult life.' *Current Directions Psychological Science*, Vol 4 (4), 99–104.

Salerno, S. (2005) 'Self-help books? Don't bother. They won't help.' *Times online*. 8th August 2005. www.timesonline.co.uk

Shermer, M. (2006) 'The Self-help and Actualization Movement' (SHAM) www.selfhelpwisdom.com

Sherwood, P. (2007) *Holistic Counselling: A New Vision of Mental Health*. Sophia Publications, Western Australia.

Sherwood, P. (2004) *The Healing Art of Clay Therapy*. Acer, Melbourne.

Smiles, S. (2008) www.wisdomquotes.com Accessed: 6th January 2008.

Smit, J. (1989) *How to transform Thinking, Feeling and Willing*. Hawthorn Press, Stroud.

Snelling, J. (1992) *The Buddhist Handbook*. Rider, London.

Steiner, R. (1999) *A Psychology of Body, Soul and Spirit*. Anthroposophical Press, NY.

Steiner, R. (1997) *An Outline of Esoteric Science*. Anthroposophic Press, NY.

Steiner, R. (1994a) *How to know Higher Worlds*. Anthroposophic Press, NY.

Therkleston, T. (2007) *Nursing the Human Being: An Anthroposophic Perspective*. Mercury Press, NY.

White, R. (1960) 'Competence and psychosexual stages of growth. Jones, M. (ed.) Nebraska Symposium on Motivation' *Perspectives on Motivation*, University of Nebraska Press, Lincoln. Vol 8, 97–141.

Winnicott, D. (1986) *Home is where we start from: Essays by a Psychoanalyst*. Norton, NY.

Wilber, K. (1998) *The Essential Ken Wilber*. Shambhala, Boston.

www.prosperyourmind.com Accessed: 20th December 2007.

www.selfhelpwisdom.com Accessed: 20th December 2007.

Chapter 2

Fox, B. (1990) 'Personal growth machine could trigger epileptic fits'. *New Scientist*, 28th July 2008. www.newscientist.com Accessed: 6th January 2009.

Goldstein, R. (2004) 'Drug Industry Scandal a Crisis'. *Inter Press Service Global Policy Forum* www.globalpolicy.org Accessed: 10th January 2008.

242   SEARCH FOR YOUR SELF

Jung, C. (1960) *On the nature of the Psyche*. Princeton University Press, Princeton.

Layard, R. (2005) *Happiness, Lessons from a New Science,* Penguin Press, NY.

Lievegoed, B. (1997) *Phases of Childhood*. Anthroposophical Press, NY.

Lievegoed, B. (1996) *Phases*. Anthroposphical Press, NY.

Lievegoed, B. (1985) *Man on the Threshold*. Hawthorn Press, Stroud.

Lok, To (1995) *The Prajna Paramita Heart Sutra*. Buddhist Educational Foundation, NY.

Samways, L. (1994) *Dangerous Persuaders: An Exposé of Gurus, Personal Growth Courses and Cults and how they operate in Australia*. Penguin, Melbourne.

Sheldon, K. and Kasser, T. (2001) 'Getting older, getting better? Personal strivings and psychological maturity across the life span.' Developmental Psychology, Vol 37 (4), 491–501.

Sherwood, P. (2007) *Holistic Counselling: A New Vision of Mental Health*. Sophia Publications, Western Australia.

Steiner, R. (1997) *An Outline of Esoteric Science*. Anthroposophic Press, NY.

Steiner, R. (1994) *How to know Higher Worlds*. Anthroposophic Press, NY.

Thich Naht Hanh (1987) *Being Peace*. Parallax Press, California.

Van De Berg, A. (ed.) (1990) *Rock Bottom*. Hawthorn Press, Stroud.

Van Schaik, S. (1990) 'Could threshold experiences cause drug use?' In: Van De Berg, A. (ed.), *Rock Bottom*, Hawthorn Press, Stroud.

Chapter 3

Eiden, B. (2002) 'Application of post-Reichian body psychotherapy: A chiron perspective.' In: Staunton, T. (ed.), *Body Psychotherapy*, Brunner-Routledge, UK. pp. 27–55.

Gendlin, E. (1974) 'Client centred and experiential psychotherapy.' In: Wexler and Rice (eds.), *Innovations in client centred Therapy*. Wiley, NY.

Grof, S. (1975) *Realms of the Human Unconscious.* Souvenir Press, London.

Hawkins, D. (2002) *Power versus Force: The Hidden Determinants of Human Behaviour.* Hay House, California.

Lowen, A. (1990) *The Spirituality of the Body*, Macmillan, NY.

Pert, C. (1999) *Molecules of Emotion: The Science behind Mind-Body Medicine.* Touchstone, NY.

Pierrakos, J. (1990) *Core Energetics.* Life Rhythm Publications, California.

Reich, W. (1973) *The Function of the Orgasm.* Souvenir Press, London.

Sherwood, P. (2007) *Holistic Counselling: A New Vision of Mental Health.* Sophia Publications, Western Australia.

Sherwood, P. (2004) *The Healing Art of Clay Therapy.* Acer, Melbourne.

Staunton, T. (ed.) (2002) *Body Psychotherapy.* Brunner-Routledge, UK.

Tagar, Y. (1996) *Philophonetics: Love of Sound.* Persephone Publications, Melbourne.

Totton, N. (2003) *Body Psychotherapy.* Open University Press, Philadelphia.

Vick, P. (2002) 'Psycho-spiritual body psychotherapy'. In: Staunton, T., *Body Psychotherapy*. Brunner-Routledge, UK. pp.113–47.

Chapter 4

Bohart, A. and Tallman, K. (1998) 'The person as active agent in experiential therapy.' In: Greenberg, L., Watson, J. and Lietaer, G. (eds.) *Handbook of Experiential Psychotherapy*. Guildford Press, NY.

Brown, J. (1999) 'Boundary violation: A practitioner's personal account.' *Psychotherapy in Australia*, Vol 6 (1), 116–20.

Changeling http://faeryshaman.co.uk/shaman/quotes.html Accessed: 7th January 2008.

Frankl, V. (1965) *The Doctor and the Soul: From Psychotherapy to Logotherapy*. Knopf, NY.

Gibney, P. (2003) *The Pragmatics of Therapeutic Practice*. Psych-oz Publications, Melbourne.

Hariman, J. (ed.) (1984) *Does Psychotherapy really help people?* Charles C. Thomas, Illinois.

Jones, C., Shillito-Clarke, C. and Syme, G. (2000) *Questions of Ethics in Counselling and Therapy*. Open University Press, Buckingham.

McBride, N. and Tunnecliffe, M. (2002) *Risky Practices: A Counsellor's Guide to Risk Management in Private Practice*. Bayside, Western Australia.

Meichenbaum, D. (1991) 'Evolution of cognitive behavioural therapy.' In: Zeig, J. (ed.), *The Evolution of Psychotherapy II*. Brunner/Matzel, NY.

Miller, S. (ed.) (1999) *The Heart and Soul of Change: A Handbook of Common Factors in Treatment*, APA Press, Washington.

Minuchin, S. (1974) *Families and Family Therapy*. Harvard University Press, Cambridge.

Pierrakos, J. (1987) *Core Energetics*. Life Rhythm Publications, California.

Pierrakos, J. (1975) *The Core Energetic Process in Group Therapy*. Institute for the New Age in Man, NY.

Roger, C. (1998) 'A therapist's view of the good life: The fully functioning person.' In: Kirschenbaum and Henderson (eds.) *The Carl Roger's Reader*, Constable, London, pp.409–29.

Rogers. C. (1978) *On Personal Power*. Constable, London.

Rowan, J. (1990) *The Transpersonal: Psychotherapy and Counselling*. Routledge, London.

Sherwood, P. (2001) 'Client experience in psychotherapy: What harms and heals.' *Indo-Pacific Journal of Phenomenology*, Vol 2, September, 56–76.

Syme, G. (2003) *Dual Relationships in Counselling and Psychotherapy*. Sage, UK.

Welwood, J. (ed.) (1983) *Awakening the Heart: East-West Approaches to Psychotherapy and the Healing Relationship*. New Science Library, London.

Tacey, D. (2003) *The Spirituality Revolution: The Emergence of Contemporary Spirituality*. Harper Collins, Sydney.

Weir, M. (2000) *Complementary Medicine: Ethics and the Law*. Prometheus Publications, Brisbane.

Chapter 5

Clark, T. and Salaman, G. (1996) 'The Management Guru as Organizational Witchdoctor.' *Organization*, Vol 3 (1). 85–107.

Dawson, F. (2006) 'Psychopathologies and the attribution of Charisma: A critical introduction to the psychology of charisma and the explanation of violence in New Religious Movements'. *Nova Religio*, Vol 10 (2), 3–28.

DuPertois, L. (1986) 'How people recognize Charisma: The case of Darshan in Radhasoami and Divine Light Mission'. *Sociological Analysis*, Vol 47 (2), 111–124.

Katz, M. (1999) 'Internet Gurus, Prominent Internet Professionals'. *Audiencia Cultura I* Xarxa, 157–89.

La Barre, W. (1980) *Culture in Context*. Duke University Press, Durham, NC.

McIlwain, D. (2006) 'The charisma of fallible leaders and the limits of self-help'. *Australian Review of Public Affairs*, www.australianreview.net Accessed: 1st May 2006.

Samways, L. (1994) *Dangerous Persuaders: An Exposé of Gurus, Personal Growth Courses and Cults and How They Operate in Australia*. Penguin, Melbourne.

Satchidananda, S. (1979) *Guru and Disciple*. Integral Yoga Publications, Connecticut.

Urban, H. (1996) 'Zorba the Buddha, capitalism, charisma and Cult of Bhagwan Shree Rajneesh'. *Religion*, Vol 26 (2), 161–82.

Weber, M, (1968) 'Charisma and its transformation'. In: Roth, G. and Wittich, C. (eds.), *Economy and Society*, Bedminster, NY.

Wright, S. (1989) *Leaving the Cults: The Dynamics of Defection*. Society for the Scientific Study of Religion, NY.

Yogananda, Swami (1946) *Autobiography of a Yogi*. Free Press, California.

Chapter 6

Bell, D. (1979) *The Cultural Contradictions of Capitalism*. Heinmann Educational, London.

Cock, P. (1979) *Alternative Australia*. Quartet, Melbourne.

Kohut, H. (1977), *The Restoration of Self*. International Universities Press, NY.

Lasch, C. (1979) *The Culture of Narcissism*. Norton Company, NY.

Layard, R. (2005) *Happiness: Lessons from a New Science*. Penguin Press, NY.

Lievegoed, B. (1985) *Man on the Threshold*. Hawthorn Press, Stroud.

Lyons, A. and Truzzi, M. (1991) *The Blue Sense*. Warner Books, NY.

Reiser, M., Ludwig, L., Sace, S. and Wagner, C. (1979) 'An evaluation of the use of psychics in the investigation of major crimes'. *Journal of Police Science and Administration*, Vol 7 (1), 18–25.

'What is a Psychic?' www.psychic.com.au Accessed: 10th January 2008.

Wiseman, R. and West, D. (1996) 'An experimental test of psychic detection'. *Journal of the Society for Psychical Research*, Vol 61 (842), 34–45.

Zygmunt, J. (1972) 'Movements and motives: Some unresolved issues in the psychology of social movements'. *Human Relations*, Vol 15, 449–67.

Chapter 7

Bedson, P. (2005) 'The healing power of presence'. *Healthy Living magazine*. The Gawler Foundation, Melbourne.

Capra, F. (1975) *The Tao of Physics: An Exploration of the Parallels Between Modern Physics and Eastern Mysticism*. Tambala Publications, Berkeley.

SEARCH FOR YOUR SELF

Clow, A. (2007) *The Mayan Code. Time Acceleration and Awakening the World Mind.* Bear Press and Company, Vermont.

Clow. A. (1995) *The Pleiadian Agenda: A new Cosmology for the Age of Light.* Bear Press and Company, Vermont.

Fodor, N. (2008) 'Encyclopaedia of Psychic Science'. www. spiritwritings.com Accessed: 10th January 2008.

Goodling, A. and Parker, A. (2001) 'Finding Psi in the paranormal: Psychometric measures used in research on paranormal. Beliefs /experiences in research on psi-ability.' *European journal of parapsychology,* Vol 16, 73–101.

Leshan, L. (2003) *The Medium, the Mystic and the Physicist,* Helios Press, NY.

Lievegoed, B. (1997) *Phases of Childhood.* Anthroposophical Press, NY.

Lievegoed, B. (1996) *Phases: The Spiritual Rhythms in Adult Life.* Anthroposophical Press, NY.

Lievegoed, B. (1985) *Man on the Threshold.* Hawthorn Press, Stroud.

Newport, F. and Strausberg, M. (8th June 2001) 'Americans' Belief in psychic and paranormal Phenomena is up over last Decade'. Report by *the Gallup Organization.* www. gallup.com/poll/4483/americans-belief-psychic-paranormal-phenomena-over-last-decade.aspx

O'Keefe, C. and Wiseman, R. (2005) 'Testing alleged mediumship: Method and results'. *British Journal of Psychology,* Vol 96, 165–79.

Roe, C.A. (1998) 'Belief in the paranormal and attendance at psychic readings'. *Journal of the American Society for Psychical Research,* Vol 92 (1), 25–71.

Steiner, R. (1922) *Theosophy.* Rudolf Steiner Press, NY.

Steiner, R. (1994) *How to know Higher Worlds: A Modern Path of Initiation.* Anthroposophic press, NY

Steiner, R. (1999). *A Psychology of Body, Soul & Spirit.* Anthroposophic Press, NY.

Thich Naht Hahn (1987) *Being Peace.* Parallex, Berkley.

Tuttle, H. (n.d., approx 1900) *Mediumship and its Laws: Its Conditions and Cultivation.* Kessinger Publishing, Montana.

Wiseman, R, and Morris, R.L (1995) *Guidelines for testing Psychic Claimants.* Prometheus Books, NY.

Chapter 8

Benavides, G. (1998) 'Modernity'. In: Taylor, M. (ed.), *Critical Terms for Religious Studies*, Chicago University Press, Chicago. pp.186–204.

Halifax, J. (ed.) (1979) *Shamanic Voices: A Survey of Visionary Narratives.* Penguin, London.

Hamayon, R. (1998) 'Ecstasy or the west-dreamt Siberian shaman'. In: Wautischer, H. (ed.), *Tribal Epistemologies: Essays in the Philosophy of Anthropology*, Ashgate, UK. pp.175–87.

Harner, M. (1980) *The Way of the Shaman.* Harper, San Franscisco.

Harner, S. and Tyron, W. (1996) 'Psychological and Immunological Responses to Shamanic Journeying with Drumming'. *Shaman* Vol 4, (1/2), 89–97.

Harvey, G. (ed.) (2003) *Shamanism: A Reader.* Routledge and Keagan, NY.

Kehoe, A. (2000) *Shamans and Religion: An Anthropological Exploration in Critical Thinking.* Waveland Press, London.

Turner, H. (1982) 'World of the spirits'. In: Metz, W., *The World's Religions*, Lion, Herts. pp 128–32.

Von Stuckard, K. (2002) 'Re-enchanting nature: Modern western shamanism and nineteenth-century thought'. *Journal of American Academy of Religion*, Vol 70 (4), 771–800.

Walsh, R. (2001) 'Shamanic Experiences: A developmental analysis'. *Journal of Humanistic psychology*, Vol 41, 31–48.

Walsh, R. (1990) *The Spirit of Shamanism*. JP Tarcher, Los Angeles.

Chapter 9

Campbell, A. (2001) 'Mind out of time: Heroin use and the problem of boredom'. *Psychotherapy in Australia*, Vol 7 (2), 42–44.

De Alba, I., Samet, J.H. and Saitz, R. (2004) 'Burden of medical illness in drug and alcohol-dependent people without primary care'. *American Journal of Addiction*, 13, 33–45.

Dunselman, R. (1993) *In Place of Self: How Drugs work*. Hawthorn Press, Stroud.

Dunselman, R. (1990) 'What are drugs, how do they work, and what are the effects of their use?' In: Van Den Berg, A. (ed.), *Rock Bottom*, Hawthorn Press, Stroud.

Metzner, R. (2005) 'Psychedelic, psychoactive and addictive drugs and states of consciousness'. In: Earleywine, M. (ed.) (2005) *Mind Altering Drugs: The Science of Subjective Experience*, Oxford Press, Oxford.

Frankl, V. (1963) Lasch, I. (trans.) *Man's Search for Meaning: An Introduction to Logotherapy*. Beacon Press, Boston

Greenfield, R. (2006) *Timothy Leary: A Biography*. Harcourt Press.

Leary, T (1965) 'A New behaviour change programme using psilocybin'. *Psychotherapy: theory, research and practice*, Vol 2 (2) pp61–72

Lievegoed, B. (1985) *Man on the Threshold*. Hawthorn Press, Stroud.

Mertens, J.R, Lu, Yun W., Parthasarathy, S., Moore, C. and Weisner, C.M. (2003) 'Medical and psychiatric conditions of alcohol and drug treatment patients in an HMO'. *Archives of Internal Medicine*, 163 (20), 2511–17.

Sherwood, P. (2007) *Holistic Counselling: A New Vision for Mental Health*. Sophia Publications, Western Australia.

The National Institute on Drug Abuse. (USA). http://www.nida.nih.gov/consequences Accessed: 16th March 2008.

Van Den Berg, A. (ed.) (1990) *Rock Bottom*. Hawthorn Press, Stroud.

Van der Haar, J. (1990) 'Addiction as an aspect of the quest of self-knowledge' In: Van Den Berg, A. (ed.) *Rock Bottom*, Hawthorn Press, Stroud.

Van Gerven, M. (1990) 'What is addiction?' In: Van Den Berg, A. (ed.) *Rock Bottom*, Hawthorn Press, Stroud.

Van Lelieveld, C. (1990) 'How can we understand the causes of drugs?' In: Van Den Berg, A. (ed.) *Rock Bottom*, Hawthorn Press, Stroud.

Van Schaik, S. (1990) 'Could threshold experiences cause drug use?' In: Van Den Berg, A. (ed.) *Rock Bottom*, Hawthorn Press, Stroud.

Vogt, F. (2002) *Addiction's Many Faces*. Hawthorn Press, Stroud.

Chapter 10

Barks, C. (trans.) (2007) *Rumi: Bridge to the Soul: Journeys into the Music and Silence of the Heart*. Harper Collins, NY.

Bogart, G. (1991) 'Meditation and psychotherapy: A review of the literature'. *The American Journal of Psychotherapy.* http://www.buddhanet.net/medpsch.htm Accessed: August 2008.

Conze, E., Horner, I., Snellgrove, D., Waley, A. (eds.) (1954) *Buddhist Texts through the Ages.* Shambala, Massachusetts.

Dawson, G. (2000) *Buddhism and psychotherapy.* Bodhi Leaf, Vol 22 (3), 3–14.

Deurr, N. (2004) *A powerful Silence: The Role of Meditation and other Contemplative Practices in American Life and Work.* Center for Contemplative Mind in Society, Northampton, MA.

Ellison, K. (2006) 'Mastering Your Own Mind'. *Psychology Today,* Vol 39 (5), 72–77.

Epstein, M. (1995) *Thoughts without a Thinker.* Basic Books, NY.

Hawkins, M. (2003) 'Effectiveness of the Transcendental Meditation programme in criminal rehabilitation and substance abuse recovery: A review of the research'. *Journal of Offender Rehabilitation,* Vol 36 (1–4), 47.

Kabat-Zinn, J. (2005) *Wherever you go, there you are: Mindfulness Meditation in Everyday Life.* Hyperion, NY.

Kabat-Zinn J. (1990) *Full Catastrophe Living: How to cope with Stress, Pain and Illness using Mindfulness Meditation.* Bantam, NY.

Kornfield, J. (1988) 'Meditation and Psychotherapy: A plea for integration'. *Inquiring Mind,* 10–11.

Meadows, G. (2004) 'A randomized controlled Trial of Mindfulness based Cognitive Therapy and Adherence Therapy for the Prevention of Relapse and Recurrence of Depression in Primary Care'. www.beyondblue.org.au Accessed: 22nd June 2004.

Queen, S. (2000) *Engaged Buddhism in the West*. Wisdom Publications, Boston.

Rubin, J. (1996) *Psychotherapy and Buddhism: Towards an Integration*. Plenum Press, NY.

Sherwood, P. (2004) *The Buddha is in the Street: Engaged Buddhism in Australia*. Edith Cowan University, Bunbury.

Shure, M., Christopher, J., Christopher, S. (2008) 'Mind-body medicine and the art of self-care: Teaching mindfulness to counselling students though yoga, meditation and qigong'. *Journal of Counselling and Growth*, Vol 86 (1), 47–56.

Walsh, R. and Shapiro, S. (2006) 'The meeting of meditation disciplines and western psychology: A mutually enriching dialogue'. *American Psychologist*, Vol 61 (3), 227–39.

Walsh, R. and Vaughan, F. (eds.) (1993) *Paths beyond Ego*. Tarcher, Los Angeles.

Welwood, J. (ed.) (1983) *Awakening the Heart: East-West Approaches to Psychotherapy and the Healing Relationship*. Shambala, Boulder.

Wilber, K., Engler, J. and Brown, D. (eds.) (1986) *Transformations of Consciousness: Conventional and Contemplative Perspectives on Growth*. Shambala, Boston.

Chapter 11

Barry, C., Grafeman, S., Adler, K. and Pickard, D. (2007) 'The relationships among narcissism, self-esteem and delinquency in a sample of at-risk adolescents'. *Journal of Adolescence*, Vol 30, 933–42.

Bhagavad Gita, http://www.bhagavad-gita.org/index-english. html Accessed: 17th March 2008.

Chatterjee, A. and Hambrick, D. (2007) 'It's all about me:

Narcissistic chief executive officers and their effects on company strategy and performance'. *Administrative Science Quarterly*, Vol 52 (3), 351.

Hotchkiss, S. (2005) 'Key concepts in the theory and treatment of narcissistic phenomena'. *Clinical Social Work Journal*, Vol 33 (2), 127–44.

Horton, R., Bleau, G. and Drwecki, B. (2006) 'Parenting Narcissus: What are the links between parenting and narcissism?' *Journal of Personality*, Vol 74 (2), 345–76.

Imbesi, L. (1999) 'The making of a narcissist'. *Clinical Social Work Journal*, Vol 27 (1), 41–45.

Lasch, C. (1979) *The Culture of Narcissism: An Age of Diminishing Expectations*. Warner Books, NY.

Lowen, A. (1997) *Narcissism: Denial of the True Self*. Simon and Schuster, NY.

McIlwain, D. (2006) 'The charisma of fallible leaders and the limits of self-help'. *Australian Review of Public Affairs*, www.australianreview.net Accessed: 1st May 2006.

Salerno, S. (2005) *SHAM Self-help and Actualization Movement: How the Gurus of the Self-Help Movement make us helpless*. Nicholas Brealey, London.

Samways, L. (1994) *Dangerous Persuaders: An Exposé of Gurus, Personal Growth Courses and Cults and how they operate in Australia*. Penguin, Melbourne.

Sherwood, P. (2004) *The Healing Art of Clay Therapy*. Acer, Melbourne.

Vaknin, S. (2003) *Malignant Self-Love: Narcissism revisited*. Narcissus Publications, Skopje and Prague.

'What makes Narcissists Tick: understanding narcissistic Personality disorder' www.narcissism.Operationdoubles.com accessed 25-1-2008

Vogel, C. (2006) 'A guide to narcissism'. *Psychology Today*, Vol 39 (1), 66–74.

Chapter 12

Alexander, C., Davies, J., Dixon, M., Dillbeck, S., Druker, R., Oetzel, J., Muehlman, J. and Orme-Johnson, D. (1990) 'Growth of higher states of consciousness: Maharishi's Vedic psychology of human growth'. In: Alexander, C. and Longer, E., *Higher Stages of Human Growth: Perspectives on Adult Growth*, Oxford University Press, NY.

Burns, R. (1986) *The Self Concept: Theory, Measurement, Growth and Behaviour*. Longman, Essex.

Burtt, E. (1982) *The Teachings of the Compassionate Buddha*. Mentor, NY.

Chah, A. (1994) *A Still Forest Pool*. Theosophical House, Illinois.

Chodron, P. (2002) 'To know yourself is to forget yourself'. *Eastern Horizon*, Issue 9, 10.

Conze, E., Horner, I., Snellgrove, D. and Waley, A. (eds.) (1954). *Buddhist Texts throughout the Ages*. Shambala, Massachusetts.

Engler, J. (1984) 'Therapeutic aims in psychotherapy and meditation: Developmental stages in the representation of self'. In: Wilbur, K., Engler, J., and Brown D. (eds.), *Transformations of Consciousness: Conventional and Contemplative Perspectives on Human Growth*. Shambala, Boston, pp.17–51.

Epstein, M. (1996) *Thoughts without A Thinker*. Duckworth, London.

Geshe Tsultim Gyeltsen (2000) *Mirror of Wisdom: Teachings on Emptiness*. Thubten Dhargye Ling Publications, California.

Maslow, A. (1973) *The Farther Reaches of Human Nature.* Penguin, Melbourne.

Maslow, A. (1968) *Toward a Psychology of Being.* VanNostrad, NY.

Maslow, A. (1959) *New Knowledge in Human Values.* Gateway, Indiana.

Roshi, J. (1983) 'Where is the self?' In: Welwood, J. (ed.), *Awakening the Heart: East-West Approaches to Psychotherapy and the Healing Relationship.* Shambala, Boulder.

Rubin, J. (1996) *Psychotherapy and Buddhism: Toward an Integration.* Plenum Press, NY.

Shantiveda (2000) 'The Boddhisattva Path'. In: Kaza, S. and Kraft, K. (eds.) *Dharma Rain.* Shambala, Boston, pp.33f.

Steiner, R. (1997) *An Outline of Esoteric Science.* Anthroposophic Press, NY.

Suzuki, D. (1970) *Essays in Zen Buddhism.* Rider, London.

Thich Naht Hanh (1996) *Living Buddha, Living Christ.* Rider, London.

Wilber, K. (1983) *Eye to Eye: The Quest or the New Paradigm.* Anchor Books, NY.